The Ghost Tour of Great Britain

Yorkshire

The Ghost Tour of Great Britain

Yorkshire

with *Most Haunted's* **Richard Felix**

breedon **books** PUBLISHING

First published in Great Britain in 2005 by
The Breedon Books Publishing Company Limited
Breedon House, 3 The Parker Centre, Derby, DE21 4SZ.

ISBN 1 85983 477 9

Printed and bound by Biddles Ltd, Hardwick Industrial Estate,
King's Lynn, Norfolk.

CONTENTS

ACKNOWLEDGEMENTS

The production of this book would not have been possible
without the help and expertise of:

the other members of the Ghost Tour team,

Steve Lilley and Delicia Redfern

Nathan Fearn

and all the staff at Breedon Books in Derby

The Ghost Tour team (left to right): Steve Lilley, Delicia Redfern, Richard Felix.

PREFACE

When local historian Richard Felix opened a Heritage Centre in his home city of Derby, England, in 1992, even his far-reaching powers of perception could not have forecast how important a step he had taken.

The Heritage Centre, based in an area of the city known as St Peter's churchyard, became the starting point for Richard's innovative ghost walks and within 12 years more than 150,000 people – many of them so fascinated by the concept that they visited from America – had booked in to be scared out of their wits.

Soon the Derby ghost walks took on legendary status and were attended by scores of would-be ghost hunters. The story unfolds as ghost walkers leave the Heritage Centre and are told that they are walking over the bodies of many of the victims of the Black Death. They head down St Peter's Street towards the site of Derby's first gaol, a place of incarceration for witches, heretics and traitors. The Lock-Up Yard, the scene of the brutal murder of a policeman, is visited next. A moment's reprieve permits the ghost-hunters to partake of another kind of spirit in the Tiger Bar, in preparation for a subterranean trip down into the barrel-vaulted tunnels beneath Derby's Guildhall. The story continues as the party heads across the Market Place, then on to the Cathedral, the Shire Hall (the scene of a horrendous pressing to death in 1665), before returning to the Heritage Centre for a Ghost Hunter's Supper – for those who can stomach the feast that is!

With the success of his ghost tours in Derby it became clear to Richard Felix that a formula that worked so well in one place would probably succeed in other towns and cities across the British Isles, and so when he was approached by film producer Stephen Lilley to record a remarkable DVD series – *The Ghost Tour of Great Britain* – he jumped at the chance. It was a mammoth, time-consuming task that relied on the great British public taking the idea seriously. And they did. The intrepid pair visited every major city and well over 40 counties throughout England, Scotland, Ireland and Wales and, with incredible attention to detail, they attempted to uncover explanations for each eerie haunting, researching library archives and interviewing credible witnesses, historians, renowned psychics and parapsychologists.

As interest in the ghost walks and *The Ghost Tour of Great Britain* increased, so did Richard Felix's fame as an authority on all things paranormal. He was invited to become the resident historical expert on the hugely popular Living TV show *Most Haunted*. Appropriately, one of the places investigated by *Most Haunted* was Derby Gaol – undoubtedly one of the most haunted sites in Britain. Situated in the basement of 50/51 Friar Gate, Derby Gaol is a working museum where visitors can see the actual cells where prisoners were kept. It was used as a prison from 1756 to 1828 and, following its acquisition by Richard Felix in 1997, has been restored to its original condition. Now visitors can try paranormal investigations using the latest hi-tech ghost-hunting equipment, just as the *Most Haunted* team did on film inside the Condemned Cell. Those of a fearless disposition can even sign up for a Derby Gaol Sleepover, comprising a mini ghost walk for an hour and a half around Friar Gate, a pie and porter supper and a bar that serves all night! A medium can also be arranged to carry out séances and private readings.

This book has been written to accompany the DVD series and recounts in words and pictures the chilling accounts of paranormal experiences uncovered by Richard Felix and Steve Lilley on their groundbreaking trip, *The Ghost Tour of Great Britain*.

PART ONE

GHOSTS

AND HOW

TO FIND

THEM

RICHARD'S THEORIES ABOUT GHOSTS

As I was raised in a haunted house, you will forgive me for having well-formed ideas about the existence of ghosts. After years of study and countless fascinating experiences, some of them truly frightening, I now consider myself an expert in the paranormal.

It may surprise you to learn, therefore, that as a child the very thought of spirits, ghouls and skeletons filled me with fear and dread. I was petrified by ghosts and, to a certain extent, I still am to this day. When I was no more than four years old I was locked into garages and garden sheds by so-called friends and told that the 'Green Ghost' was going to get me. Experiences such as this only served to fuel an already fertile imagination and as a child I would refuse to stay in any building on my own and would certainly never walk past a churchyard alone or even walk upstairs without someone's hand to hold. I spent many a night as a youngster lying wide awake beneath my bedclothes, waiting for a demonic being to stride into my bedroom, pull back the bedclothes and reveal its hideous face. Of course this never happened, but perhaps my way of facing up to my fears was to attempt to discover all I possibly could about how and why spirits haunt places.

In the early 1990s I started to conduct ghost walks around Derby – and 12 years later well over 150,000 people had been on a ghost tour of my home city. Derby's location, almost in the centre of the country, has underlined its great importance for almost 2,000 years and contributed to its prosperity. It has always been a crossing of the ways and was the scene of the last hanging, drawing and quartering to be carried out in England, the result of the last rebellion against the Crown to take place in this country.

However, every region of these isles has its own folklore and legends and in recognition of this Stephen Lilley and I embarked on *The Ghost Tour of Great Britain*. In less than three years we visited nearly every county in the land, looking for ghosts, talking to people who have seen ghosts and visiting haunted places. My experiences as an expert on the popular *Most Haunted* TV programme have broadened my horizons still further and put me in direct contact with the scariest places in Great Britain and beyond. Even today, however, I am still learning and remain grateful to the

folklorists and parapsychologists who continually surprise me with their thoughts and theories.

In this book, you will read chilling tales of hauntings, but I will also attempt to pass on, from my own experiences, the knowledge and details of the equipment you need to detect paranormal activity yourself. In short, everything you need to know to become a ghost-hunter.

First, however, you need to understand what a ghost is.

Some parapsychologists don't believe in life after death and put hauntings down to the influence of the living, not the dead. They attribute unexplained events to Extra Sensory Perception (ESP) – the psychic powers of living individuals who have the ability, for example, to move objects.

We are taught from an early age that we *can't* do certain things. If a door opens by itself, a spoon bends without any force being applied to it or a glass on a mantelpiece suddenly shatters, as adults we look for a logical explanation. Those who believe in ESP say that this desire to explain away inexplicable events is no more than a safety valve – far better to be a sceptic than attribute strange happenings to the power of the mind and run the risk of being ridiculed. And at least ESP and the idea of telepathic understanding between living creatures is a more comfortable theory to swallow than the spectre of the dead being trapped on earth as punishment for terrible crimes or through the tragedy and pain of an unexpected demise.

The idea of sharing our world – sometimes our own homes – with the spirits of dead people is uncomfortable to say the least, but I have met hundreds of sane, sober individuals who swear they have encountered a ghost. Intrigued? Well, before you read on, please make a note of the Richard Felix Rules of Ghost Hunting. First, you have to be an enthusiast. Second, you need to be a detective, and third, most certainly a sceptic. You have to explore all avenues when you look into a ghost's history and get to the bottom of the *reason* for the haunting.

For many, that would be enough. However, I passionately believe the ultimate aim of the ghost-hunter is to ask: 'How can I help?' If you're looking for nothing more than the cheap thrill of a scary experience, go and watch a horror movie. I feel that there's a responsibility attached to ghost-hunting. If an animal lover tracks down a caged gorilla, does he simply take a photograph of the sad ape and walk away? No, that's not enough – the final act has to be to release the creature from its pain. It is therefore important to understand that ghosts – whether the product of the living or the dead – haunt places for different reasons and I believe that there are at least five distinct types.

The dead returning

This is where a spirit is seeking some kind of 'closure', as our American friends might say. It can interact, is aware of its environment and knows you are there – it's a conscious entity that can even speak to you. To me, this is the most frightening type of ghost, but what's the reason for its existence? The basic premise is that while the spirit of a dead person remains on earth, the soul moves on to its eternal reward. So maybe our interactive ghosts have business on earth they haven't concluded or are somehow trapped and can't move on to where good souls go.

In the Middle Ages there was a strong belief in Purgatory – a state in between heaven and hell. Quite often human bones are found where ghosts have been seen for a number of years and a common theory is that troubled souls haunt the earth because they weren't buried properly. The way we depart this life isn't something most of us think too deeply about these days, but in bygone times people craved a decent burial. Could denial of the Last Rites or bitterness that their bones were interred in ground that was not consecrated create the energy of a troubled ghost, stubbornly waiting for a proper burial?

I spoke recently to a Cornish woman who told me that through the Church's influence in the Middle Ages and its warnings of eternal damnation, souls that had done bad deeds in life were simply too afraid to move on, so instead hovered on earth as ghosts.

This theory may help to explain why we don't see many modern ghosts – there was more fear in the past of the punishment for sins in death, hence the reluctance of some to take the step into the afterlife. Perhaps these days we are more relaxed about our wrong-doings and don't believe they have to be paid for when we die?

Some ghosts apparently don't have any choice about whether or not they move on to another place. We have long been told that individuals who have committed terrible crimes are condemned to walk this earth for eternity, repenting their sins. Marley's ghost in Charles Dickens's *A Christmas Carol* warns Scrooge to mend his ways, or face the prospect of dragging in death the heavy chains he has forged link by link throughout his corrupt life.

The fact that these interactive ghosts represent the dead returning and the spirits of real people – entities with intelligence – makes them difficult to track down. Why would a self-respecting ghost with the ability to interact allow itself to be nailed by a gang of hi-tech ghost-hunters wielding laser temperature readers?

The apparition

If you could take a camcorder and video player back in time 200 years, imagine how staggered the people of early 19th-century Britain would be at your ability to play back on a screen a particular event you had just recorded.

So why are we shocked today by the idea of a traumatic event, perhaps a terrible premature death, somehow recording itself naturally into rock, brickwork, or even soil? Stone in particular is an ideal recording medium because it contains silica, and it's my belief that the energy emanates out of the stone.

I believe electronic impulses emanate from the brain in the moments before death takes place, creating energy that imprints itself into the fabric of the location. When atmospheric conditions are right, the image created by this energy replays the scene. That's why you see an apparition as it was just before the person died, but it's no more real than watching John Wayne in an old cowboy movie. The Duke long ago rode off into the sunset to that big ranch in the sky – it's his image you see and hear on video and it's impossible for him to interact with you. The same can be said for apparitions.

The tragic scene is played out again and again, but this ghost can't interact – there's no sense of the apparition being aware of the living. Just like a favourite videotape that is played too often, apparitions tend to fade through time. There are stories of ghostly hauntings that have become less distinct down the years, starting out, for example, as a red lady in the 18th century, changing to a pink lady in the 19th century, then to a white lady in the 20th century before becoming no more than a pillar of light accompanied by the sound of footsteps.

Telepathic projection

Like the apparition, this ghost is created by a moment of crisis. We've all heard stories of the woman who sees the image of her husband stranded on a mountain or a soldier appearing to his family moments before he is killed in the trenches.

These are classic examples of the telepathic understanding between people who love each other. In some cases the person who appears as a 'ghost' doesn't actually die, because their appearance prompts a loved-one to summon help. We have all experienced that nagging voice in our head that tells us to visit a relative or friend we know is sick. It's a telepathic experience linked to high emotion.

Phantasm

This is a bizarre apparition that, some would say, proves that ghosts are as much to do with the living as the dead. In the 1888 Census of Hallucinations, a huge survey, the Society for Psychical Research interviewed people throughout the British Isles and Northern France and came up with a surprising statistic. It was discovered that where those questioned were actually able to identify the ghost they had seen, half of the 'ghosts' were still alive and in no danger at the time they were seen! Phantasms are created by another form of telepathy, where an individual, though alive, somehow places an image of himself elsewhere. Far-fetched? Well I have a first-hand account of a baker who, after he had retired, was seen by the new owner of the business as an apparition going about his duties in the bakery. The new owner assumed that he had seen a ghost and that the old baker must be dead. However, on further investigation he discovered that the old man was very much alive, but had little to do in retirement. Consequently he spent most of his time in solitude, daydreaming about his old job. In doing this he somehow provoked the ghostly image of himself to appear at his beloved bakery to be witnessed by the new owner.

Poltergeist

Poltergeists represent a big group of ghosts. There are two contrasting schools of thought on exactly what makes a poltergeist. The name comes from the mediaeval German words *polte* (noisy) and *geist* (ghost). Once again the definition of this ghost comes down to a battle between the living and the dead. One side of the argument believes poltergeists are mischievous, sometimes malevolent, spirits who inhabit a particular place, often a room. The other side goes with the theory of Recurrent Spontaneous Psycho Kinesis, or RSPK for short. They believe that living people, for reasons we don't understand, use the power of their own minds to affect their environments.

Scary movies have given many people a very definite idea of what poltergeists do. We have been drip-fed an image of mischievous spirits throwing objects across rooms, but poltergeist hauntings tend to be more measured than the cinematic interpretation suggests. More regularly they start with a scratching sound and then move on to the odd loud bang, progressing to unpleasant smells. Eventually objects start to move – not initially by floating across a room, but in an annoying way. A set of house keys you always leave on the kitchen table disappears, you hunt high and low and half an hour later you find them – exactly where you left them.

Then come phenomena known as 'small object displacement'. Everyday objects disappear from a room and reappear in a different place. The next stage of a poltergeist haunting is that unusual items appear from nowhere. Old wooden toys, teddy bears, and, at its most grisly, human bones, have all been reported as appearing in rooms. Eventually poltergeist activity progresses to the classic image of objects flying across a room. It's interesting to note though that objects in these reported cases are said to float in straight lines, rather than going up and down in an arc the way they would if you or I threw something in the air and let gravity take charge.

I have very seldom spoken to anyone who has been damaged physically or mentally by ghosts – nor have I heard of poltergeist activity resulting in objects actually hitting anyone. I believe poltergeist activity isn't either mischievous or malevolent, but a call for help. The longest poltergeist incidence I have encountered is a year, but more usually it's a matter of weeks or months.

Filming one episode of *Most Haunted*, our camera captured a teddy bear flying across a room where a child had died many years before.

It seems that poltergeists focus either on a particular person or on a particular place. I have spoken to parapsychologists who have totally sealed off a room where poltergeist activity had been reported. They left a camera running and there was absolutely no possible way the room could be interfered with by any living being. They waited outside and within a minute heard a huge smashing sound. Running into the room, they found the camera pointing at the floor and a teddy bear, last seen on a sofa, sitting with its paws up in front of the fire, as if to warm itself against the cold.

Quite often, poltergeist cases seem to have a living agent. It's normally people who are highly intelligent, creative and imaginative, possibly disturbed by family issues. It is claimed that emotionally charged individuals troubled, for example, by the onset of puberty, cause some poltergeist experiences. That is why it is so important to map out family relationships and areas where an individual might be emotionally charged before diving in with theories and solutions. Where poltergeist activity results from one person's emotional state, the issue needs to be treated with sensitivity and respect. Sometimes a far more sensible alternative to chasing the poltergeist is recommending sound medical assistance.

A GUIDE TO GHOST-HUNTING

If you regularly tune in to the *Most Haunted* TV show, you'll see us using all manner of sophisticated ghost-hunting equipment. There really are some superb ghost-hunting aids on the market these days, and I'd advise you to examine these hi-tech units if you are looking to back up investigation successes with scientific evidence.

However, when starting out as a ghost-hunter you can, if you wish, get away with pretty basic equipment, much of it to be found around the house.

A **torch** is essential and **candles** are useful too because in addition to giving soft light they can detect movements and draughts. Another 'must have' is a **tape recorder** or **Dictaphone**. A useful rule with regard to taping sound is not to leave your recorder running – it's painstaking and ultimately unrewarding to listen back to hours of tape after a ghost-hunting session. Much better to use your tape recorder only when you have asked your ghost a question – such as the classic 'Is anybody there?' Then switch on your recorder and leave it on for two or three minutes and you could get some very good results.

You can get away with an everyday **thermometer** to gauge sudden drops in temperature, but better still is a **laser thermometer**, which detects the temperature at exactly the point its red scan light hits and gives a reading on a handheld gauge.

Tape – such as household masking tape – is useful for taping off areas of activity or windows. A piece of **thread** can also be useful to section off small areas, such as a tabletop.

To assist in monitoring the movement of trigger objects, items that move during poltergeist activity, an upturned **transparent case** can come in handy. Try a plastic fish tank – and I'd recommend an empty one! Putting trigger objects underneath plastic makes for a more scientific examination of item movement because it eradicates the possibility of anything being moved by natural factors, such as draughts or wind.

In the absence of digital recording equipment, something as basic as a piece of **graph paper** at least gives you the opportunity to map out items on a table or in a room before and after a poltergeist haunting.

Dowsing rods are ghost-hunting implements you need to acquire a relationship with, and a feel for, quite literally! In simple terms the rods are two pieces of thin rigid wire, the consistency of a typical Firework Night sparkler and around 18 inches long in each case. Place each rod lightly between the first and second finger of each hand and, with fists clenched and facing away from the body, and elbows slightly bent, hold the rods out horizontally in front of you approximately six inches apart. Try them out in any space, particularly one where a haunting has been reported, and simply ask the rods to give you 'yes' and 'no' answers to questions. I believe you get a 'yes' when the rods cross inwards and a 'no' when they angle away from each other. If you ask if a spirit is in the room you are in and the answer is 'yes', you can then ask the rods to point in the direction of the spirit. Patience and concentration is needed, but in my experience dowsing rods really do work. I don't know *how* they work but my gut feeling is that it's something to do with the power of the mind transmitting itself through the body and into the rods. Ask me for a scientific explanation and I can offer none, but my own personal experience of using rods is both positive and genuine.

If and when you really catch the ghost-hunting bug you might want to invest in some of the incredibly sophisticated pieces of state-of-the-art equipment now on the market. Such is the interest that there are companies such as the British-based Spectral Electronics that now deal exclusively in ghost-hunting aids.

The **Electro-Magnetic Field (EMF) meter** has been used for several years now by ghost-hunters and by paranormal investigators. This hand-held machine, not much bigger than a TV remote control unit, can detect electro-magnetic presence in the fabric of buildings; useful when investigating, for example, regular reported sightings of an apparition in the same place. The latest generation of EMF meters, developed specifically for paranormal investigators, are ingenious because they filter out everyday electrical charges such as mains frequencies. With a pair of normal headphones you can also measure variations in electro-magnetic energies recorded by the meter.

The **Ultra-Sonic Unit** is pretty new on the market. In look and feel it is similar to an EMF meter with a display and an audio connection. Ultra-Sonic Units measure acoustic energies in ultrasound regions at frequencies of 20khz and above, a range of sound that bats and, significantly, dogs can hear, but way beyond normal human hearing. Animals generally seem more sensitive to paranormal activity than we humble humans and devices such as the Ultra-Sonic Unit help us to redress the balance. Previously some ghost-hunters would take dogs on investigations because they seemed to be able to pick up things that humans couldn't. With the headphone connection you can monitor high-frequency sounds and, if you wish, record them onto your Dictaphone. Some of the more advanced paranormal investigation groups have even developed computer programs that enable users to store and interpret information using sounds recorded through Ultra-Sonic Units. These programs are available as free downloads on the Internet and can display spectrum analysis ranges that show, for example, energies recorded in different frequencies. So Ultra-Sonic Units do so much more than simply replicating the sensitivity of dogs, and the real beauty of them of course is you don't have to take them out for walks!

The **Negative-Ion Detector** is another 21st-century phenomenon. The low-light infrared filming we carry out on *Most Haunted* often shows up orbs, small objects that seem to fly through the air like tiny flying saucers. These orbs are believed to have some relation to high voltage or static electricity, a side effect of which is a surplus of negative ions. You can create your own electro-magnetic field through the old trick of rubbing a balloon against a jumper, creating an energy that allows the balloon to stick to a ceiling. This is the same type of energy picked up by Negative-Ion Detectors, which give out an audible beep to indicate activity.

Interviewing technique is also crucial, despite the availability of modern-day equipment that can make the business of ghost-hunting easier and ultimately more exciting. Investigators of paranormal activity must be prepared to talk to people who have witnessed a haunting when amassing evidence. It is essential therefore to develop an effective interviewing style. Devoting hour upon hour of your own time to ghost stakeouts is all very well, but it is always important to factor in the experiences of other people who have personal accounts to tell of activity in a particular case. It is rather like a detective cracking a criminal case: having first-hand evidence is fine, but to prove your case you need to accumulate witness statements. For these statements to be as effective as possible, like a police detective, you also need to develop a good interviewing technique. Let your subjects do the talking, prompt them with open-ended questions and gently but firmly ask them to stick to the facts of what they have personally seen or heard, not what they have been told by others.

Always record your interviews on a tape recorder or Dictaphone. Ask permission of your subject first of course, and respect their privacy, but recording interviews is important because it enables you to concentrate not only on what is being said, but on the *way* it is being said. Our intuition helps us form an impression of whether someone is speaking sincerely or lying through their teeth. Witnesses' body language will often either give them away or underline their credibility. If you are convinced by the sincerity of your witness the next step is to listen back to the tape and make a full transcript. This is where you, as a detective, must take a sceptical view of the evidence. If a particular witness informs you, for example, that a door in a particular building regularly slams shut for no reason, then look for a logical explanation. Is the activity caused by a through-draught that occurs naturally when another door is opened elsewhere in the house? If a witness reports the smell of tobacco in a particular room at certain times and attributes this to the presence of a pipe-smoking ghost, could it in fact be more to do with temperature changes inducing an odour in paintwork, plaster or old floorboards? Could the sound of ghostly footsteps be nothing more sinister than your neighbours in the house next door, movement in the rooms above or even thermostatically controlled central heating kicking in with a rumble and a thud?

In Tutbury Castle there's a 17th-century costume presented on a shop window-style mannequin that appears to sway entirely on its own. In fact the room where this costume is displayed shares the same old floorboards as the adjoining King's Bedroom at the Castle. Although a partition wall was erected to make one room into two at some stage in the Castle's history, the effect of walking in the King's Bedroom moves the floorboards in the adjoining room and sets the mannequin moving!

Your most reliable witnesses will inevitably be people who live or work in the place where they report paranormal activity. They will be aware of everyday sounds that have a natural cause and will be able to speak to you with greater authority about happenings that are genuinely unusual. The problem with ghost hunts and people whose experiences relate to a location they are not familiar with is that every small sound or movement seems to demand an explanation. It's far better to rely on the witness statements of people who are truly familiar with the place where a ghostly presence is reported. Give particular weight to the statements of those witnesses who stick to the facts of what they have experienced rather than speculating as to the cause. If they tell you they regularly hear footsteps in the cellar followed by a loud bang, but haven't any idea what causes this phenomenon, it's a more telling observation than someone who goes on to speculate that the activity is probably caused by the ghost of an unhappy monk who hanged himself in the

15th century, because Mrs Jones in the village reckons the house was once the site of a monastery...

A **methodical approach** is crucial for ghost-hunting. Sherlock Holmes may be a fictional detective, but he was given a very factual philosophy on detection. When approaching a case he would rule out the impossible and examine what he was left with, as this, he believed, was the truth, however improbable that truth seemed.

I can testify from personal experience to the emotion attached to seeing a ghost at first-hand and the careful analysis I went through afterwards to convince myself of what I had seen. It happened in Derby Gaol, not at dead of night during a low-light ghost hunt, but in the middle of the afternoon in a kitchen when I was on my mobile phone in conversation with a friend. Through the open door of the kitchen I saw a figure, the size of a person and grey as grey, move down one of the old gaol's corridors. Although there was no drop in temperature, I sensed it as well as seeing it. By the time I got to the actual door to the corridor, it had gone.

This experience frightened me, quite a lot. However, when I recovered I then went through the process of ruling out all the naturally occurring things that might have caused its appearance. Although what I saw had a misty appearance, it wasn't smoke, it wasn't steam and it wasn't the reflection of a car's headlights. There's a theory known as 'Standing Wave' that tells us that in certain conditions extractor fans in rooms, corridors and even in computers can give off an odd acoustic effect that creates the impression of something moving fleetingly at the very edge of an individual's vision and prompts terrible feelings of fear and anxiety. However, the grey mass I saw wasn't out of the corner of my eye; it was a full-on experience and I can think of no other explanation than my having witnessed a ghost.

Here is something strange but true: while filming an episode of *Most Haunted* I saw a spoon fly through the air. I wasn't the first person to the errant spoon when it landed and my slowness off the mark on this occasion probably saved me getting my fingers burned! In some instances items subject to poltergeist activity, whether cutlery, coffee cups or other general household objects, have been found to be red hot to the touch. This I put down to the poltergeist energy created in its movement, so approach with care!

Continuing the methodical approach to all things para-normal, it is important to log examples of poltergeist activity for future reference, so always weigh the object that has apparently moved and measure how far it has travelled. This statistical information can help you prove, for example, that items of a certain weight tend to travel a certain distance in a particular room. At the very least it is information you can pass on for others to quantify. Organisations such as the Society for Psychical Research will always be happy to offer assistance provided you have facts and figures to support your questions.

Original artefacts are always good for measuring powers of perception through a simple touching and sensing test. Anyone can try it, though some, inevitably, are more sensitive than others. Here's what you do, in a group if you wish: lay the palms of your hands lightly on an artefact – anything from a sideboard to a sword – and then clear your mind completely. Try to register signals from the item you are touching; then talk about it.

Folklore is the development of history rather than hard historical fact. For example, it may be factually correct that in the Middle Ages a woman leapt to her death from the north tower of a castle after her knight husband returned early from battle to discover her with a lover. The folklore element is the tale passed down through the ages that the apparition of a white lady is seen leaping from the same tower just before midnight, or that a candle will never burn when lit in the room at the top of the tower.

So how, as a ghost-hunter, do you try to bridge the gap between folklore and fact? First, as always, gain permission from the owners of the property you intend to investigate. You may even feel it is sensible to have a member of staff of the haunted building – a curator of the castle for example – present throughout the investigation. At the very least, draw up a written agreement with the owners or trustees of the building that your investigation has been sanctioned. I would then devise experiments suitable to the environment and probably arrange a vigil where at least two people, armed with digital recording equipment, sit at the haunted site and quite literally wait for something to happen. The vigil might take the form of a small séance where you as the ghost-hunter invite spirits to make contact. Although you as the leader of this particular investigation will be fully aware of the folklore surrounding the site in question, it's probably a good idea that others in the vigil party know as little as possible and go into the experiment with few pre-conceptions.

Ensure too that **evidence** collected during the vigil is not contaminated by over-elaboration. If, for example, a member of the party sees the apparition of an old soldier walking through a wall, he should not turn to a colleague and ask: 'Did you see the old soldier walk through the wall?' The best response would be simply to ask: 'Did you see that?' The colleague then replies with a simple 'yes' or 'no', again guarding against over-elaboration that might later be construed as auto-suggestion. Importantly though, both members of the vigil should make a note of the time of the conversation and record exactly what they did or didn't see.

If you see a ghost-hunter seemingly poking himself in the eye in a moment of high excitement during a vigil, don't be alarmed! An interesting theory supported by some in this business is that a ghostly apparition is genuine if, when you press very gently on one eyeball, you see a double image for a split second. If what you are seeing is a hallucination – a product of the mind – apparently you will only see a single image.

If you have a **medium** in your party it is fascinating to record his or her verdict on contacts made during the séance. Afterwards you can check the medium's connections and findings against established historical fact.

My view is that you cannot get closer to history than actually seeing a ghost. Parapsychologists take a different angle. They prefer in the first instance to talk to people who claim to have witnessed paranormal activity rather than attempting to experience the phenomenon themselves.

Whichever approach you choose to take, be as methodical and unemotional as possible. Your body needs to listen and work in a new way, so try to rest as much as possible in the hours before the investigation takes place. You will probably be up all night, so you will need all the energy and awareness you can muster. Don't confuse your body either by treating it to large doses of alcohol or a large spicy dinner before a vigil; eat sensibly and take along snacks that will give a kick to your blood-sugar levels during the night. Remember at around three o'clock in the morning the body goes into a different mode. This is the time when most people die and most people are born, and it is also the stage during all-night vigils that you need to give your body some fuel. Be as healthy as possible in body and spirit and be aware that even something as simple as a common cold can potentially confuse an investigation. Was that the ghostly tolling of a distant bell you just heard, or a buzz in your ears brought about because you blew your nose?

Many people like to take a **psychic** or medium on a ghost hunt. Do *not* tell them where you are going. Drive them to the location yourself, giving nothing away. You then need to measure exactly how accurate the psychic is. This can be done by creating a map of the location and recording the findings of more than one psychic at each point on the map. Alternatively draw up a list of emotive words, such as 'Happy', 'Angry', 'Murder', 'Child', 'Mediaeval' and so on… and ask each psychic to ring the words they feel most appropriate to particular areas of the location. If you discover that more than one psychic logs the same emotions in the same areas, then you are accumulating useful evidence of a haunting.

I believe the vast majority of psychics have an innate ability to see something the rest of us can't detect. It's a gift in the same way as someone who has the God-given talent to play a piano without music. I also know there are some complete charlatans practising as psychics, but I believe in ghosts and I believe in the supernatural, so I have to believe in mediums.

I have a party-piece when visiting, in particular, ancient sites such as castles, which demonstrates powerfully to me the energy that emanates from stone. I have a crystal on a string that I carry around with me and I have shown tens of thousands of people on my ghost walks how an ancient stone's energy can make the crystal swing on the string of its own accord. All I do is hold the piece of string with the crystal attached in one hand, and place the palm of my other hand on the stone. Within seconds the crystal will start to move – without any assistance from me – and I can only explain this as the energy transferring itself through my body, using the power of the mind. The moment I lift my hand from the stone, the crystal's gyrating action slows down and eventually stops. I don't cheat; I don't have to, and I defy anybody to come up with an explanation for this feat that doesn't have a supernatural foundation.

Before you read on, remember that most people who see ghosts aren't frightened when they see them, because the ghosts usually look like real people. The other important thing to remember is that eight out of 10 ghost stories can be accounted for; it's the other two you need to worry about!

So sleep well, and don't have nightmares.

GLOSSARY OF GHOSTLY TERMINOLOGY

Amulet is an item that has the power to stave off ghosts and evil spirits.

Angel is something often mistaken for a ghost, but in fact is a holy and protective messenger shielding us from harm.

Animal ghosts are believed to be the spirits of animals who survive the death process. Many experts in the paranormal acknowledge the existence of animal ghosts and some investigators even believe animals have what is known as a 'collective soul'. This theory supposes that as many as half a dozen animals at one time may share just one soul.

Apparitions are recorded in the earliest pages of history. This mysterious image of a disembodied spirit can be recognised as a human or animal. They are the most rare type of ghost to capture on film. Ghostly human forms are the easiest to fake, especially with the advanced technology of computers. This makes our job even more difficult, as it is almost impossible to prove the existence of apparitions when using photographs. Ghostly apparitions of ships, trains, cars and other inanimate objects have been seen. Some are said to appear to warn of a disaster that is about to happen, while others are thought to guard sacred places. Some apparitions are not seen, they are heard, or felt.

Apport happens when a solid object appears from nowhere, with the assistance of the spirit in the company of a medium.

Astral body is the energy that separates itself from the human form but still maintains the personality and feelings of the individual. Sometimes others will see them during an out-of-body experience (OBE) or a near-death experience (NDE).

Astral plane can be described as a level of awareness in the celestial world with its own standards and occupants.

Atmospheric apparition is a visual imprint of a person that has died left to be replayed on the atmosphere.

Aura is an energy field that surrounds all living things.

Automatic writing occurs when a ghost or spirit takes control of the writer's hand and pens a message.

Banshee is a spirit that appears before a person's death to howl a mourning song and to welcome them into the afterlife. It is also Ireland's most famous ghost. The correct pronunciation of this female spirit's name is 'bean si' and she is said to associate herself with Irish families – particularly if their surname starts with the letter 'O' – and she is more likely to be seen by a third daughter. Her appearance is said to be the portent of death for a family member, announced by crying and wailing during the hours of darkness. The sound is said to be like that of two cats fighting, only much worse. The tragic relative might be thousands of miles away in another country, and the wailing can apparently be heard for several nights in succession until the actual death occurs. The woman herself appears in contrasting ways. Sometimes she is described as a strange-smelling small, ugly hag dressed in rags. At other times she appears as a young and beautiful woman in a green dress, her eyes red and swollen from constant crying. A third type of banshee has also been reported, but it is not clear whether she is young or old, as she has no clear features, with holes where her eyes should be. The common factor linking all three types is very long hair that streams out in the wind. Folklore dictates that when a banshee is disturbed by a mortal person she will not appear again while that generation lives, but will return to haunt future generations.

Bi-location describes the phenomenon where someone can be in two places at the same time.

Birds were at one time believed to be messengers of the dead – when one tapped on a window, it was said to signify that a ghost was looking for another spirit to join it. Certain birds, such as sparrows, larks and storks, were said to transport to earth the souls of people from the Guff, or 'Hall of Souls', in heaven. Other birds, especially crows, were believed to carry the spirits of humans onto the next plane of existence.

Boggart is a word used chiefly in the north of England to describe a particularly nasty type of ghost. Boggarts are said to enjoy crawling into victims' bedrooms at night and pulling the bedclothes off, slapping, pinching and biting people, especially on the feet. In appearance they are said to be truly frightening, with sharp, long and yellowing teeth.

Bogies, like the Irish banshee, are said to make a wailing noise. An unpleasant spirit with a preference for haunting children, the bogie, according to British folklore, is foul-smelling, black, short and hairy with an ugly, grinning face. Perhaps it belongs more to the language of parents, hence the warning: 'Don't be naughty, or the bogie man will get you!' Bogies were once thought to be the most powerful of ghosts, having apparently once served the Devil by doing evil deeds against mankind.

Cats, next to dogs, are the most common form of animal spirits. The ghost cat is believed to have its spooky origin in ancient Egypt where cats were often worshipped, especially at Bubastis, where many thousands of mummified cats have been excavated. Historically the Devil was believed to be able to take the form of a cat, and cats were often thought to be witches' familiars.

Cemetery lights hover over graves after dark as bluish balls of light.

Channelling is a form of spirit possession that occurs with a medium who is communicating with an unseen entity to gain wisdom or gain knowledge of future events.

Clairaudience, a skill claimed by many mediums, is when someone has the ability to hear the voices of ghosts and other sounds that are inaudible to the human ear. These disembodied voices of the dead, or other entities, normally tell of events yet to happen. Many mediums say that they can hear dead relatives passing on information from a place they call 'the Spirit World'.

Clairvoyance is being capable of seeing events in the future or past through the mind's eye. In its simplest form, clairvoyance is to 'see with sight beyond the normal human range of sight'. A clairvoyant can see visions of events that have already happened, are actually happening or are yet to happen.

Clairsentience is, some believe, a basic human instinct finely attuned and polished. If you are clairsentient, you have the ability to feel and know things that have been, are, and are yet to be.

Cold reading is done when a psychic has no prior knowledge of the sitter.

Cold spot is an area in a haunted place where the temperature drops by several degrees. Temperature can also rise in heat by several degrees, indicating the presence of a fire in the past.

Collective apparition occurs when more than one living person sees a ghost or spirit simultaneously.

Collective unconscious is a term to describe a form of analytical psychology developed by Carl Jung. It represents the collective memory of all humanity's past and is held somewhere inside the unconscious mind.

Conjure is an act to summon a spirit to manifest itself for a desired task or to answer questions.

Corpse candle is a term referring to balls of firelight that can be seen to dance above the ground.

Crisis apparition is the vision of someone that will appear during waking hours or in a dream at the moment of a crisis.

Crossroad ghosts have been reported for centuries, and no-one knows quite why. Some researchers maintain that crossroads are more likely to be haunted because of the number of suicide victims buried there. The superstition behind interring the dead at such places lies in the Christian belief that the cross is a form of protection from demons, vampires and other supernatural night creatures. This theory, however, is thrown into doubt when it is considered that excavated human remains pre-dating Christianity have been unearthed near crossroads all over the world.

Deathwatch is a strange turn of phrase connected with a species of beetle known as the deathwatch beetle, which taps on wood. Many believe the beetle can sense the approach of death and taps in acknowledgement of spirits arriving to take the soul to its next destination.

Dogs have been reported in ghost form all over the British Isles. These spectral dogs are said to vary in size and some have been described as small but with extremely large eyes. They can also be white, black, vicious or gentle. The

Lancastrians have a ghost dog known as a Striker; in Wales there is the Gwyllgi, while Derbyshire boasts Rach Hounds and Gabriel's Ghost Hounds.

Doppelganger is a German word to describe a ghost that is the double of a living person. Those who experience seeing their double are said to be heading towards misfortune in the near future. Confusingly, other investigators are adamant that the doppelganger is also an indication of good fortune, though recorded incidences of them being a good omen are rare. People associated with the haunted individual are also reported as having seen the doppelganger at a place where the living counterpart was nowhere near.

Dowsing is the skill of seeking answers and interpreting them through the use of rods or a pendulum. Dowsing is widely used as a simple but effective way of searching for such things as lost coins, water and ghosts. It is also used to conduct geophysical surveys.

Drudes are mature witches or wizards, and reports of this nightmare ghost date from ancient England. The drude is said to be well versed in the art of magic and able to cause a ghost to appear in the dreams and nightmares of their chosen victims.

Duppy is the name given to a well-known West Indian ghost said to be able to walk the earth only between the hours of dusk and cock-crow. The duppy can be summoned from its grave by an act of ceremonial magic to do the bidding of a witch. The ceremony involves mixing blood and rum together with other substances. This concoction is then thrown on the grave of one known to have been an evil person when alive, as the duppy is widely believed to be the personification of evil in a human.

Earthlights are balls of lights or variable patches of lights appearing randomly and with no explanation as to what causes them.

Ectoplasm is a strange substance said to extrude from the sweat glands, mouth, nostrils and genitals of some mediums while in a trance-like state. A solid or vaporous substance, it is produced by a medium during a trance to reach a dead person. Ectoplasm, or teleplasm, is derived from the Greek words *ektos* and *plasma*, meaning exteriorised substance. There are researchers who claim that the substance is similar to pale white tissue paper, cheesecloth, or fine silk strands that all gather together to make a human shape. Others say the substance is like human and animal tissue. Most reports of ectoplasm have been revealed to be hoaxes. Some mediums have gone to the lengths of taking cheesecloth and rigging it to drop from a part of the body (the nose, mouth or ears). Some mediums even swallowed the cheesecloth and then regurgitated it later during the séance.

Ectoplasmic mist will usually show up in a photo as a misty white cloud to indicate the presence of a spirit. The mist is not seen when the picture is taken. These mists can vary in colour from grey and black to red and even green.

Elemental spirit is a rather curious type of ghost said to be a spirit that has never existed in human form. For this reason, occultists insist they are ancient spirits representing Earth, Air, Fire and Water that predate man. Elemental spirits are often associated with haunted stretches of woodland and rivers, mountains and valleys.

Elves are spirits of nature. Spiteful creatures, they are suffering as lost souls trapped between two worlds; not evil enough to go to hell; not quite good enough to be accepted into heaven.

EMF (Electro-Magnetic Field) meter is a device that can pick up electronic and magnetic fields. It can also detect any distortions in the normal electro-magnetic field.

Entity is a term that refers to an intelligent being who is no longer inside their physical body. They have the power to provide information to all individuals who are sensitive to their vibrations.

ESP (Extra Sensory Perception) represents an ability to gather information beyond the five human senses.

EVP (Electrical Voice Phenomenon or Electrical Visual Phenomenon) is a method by which a spirit's voice is detected by means of a recording device. It is also possible to pick up visual images of a known dead person on computer and TV screens, even when they are not switched on.

Exorcism is a religious ceremony where an attempt is made to expel a spirit that may have taken up residence inside a house or a human being. The ceremony usually involves a clergyman such as a priest, often specially trained, who will say prayers and repeat loud exhortations, often burning candles and sprinkling holy water while incense is burned. Exorcism is actually a modern version of the old Christian practice of excommunication – the rite of 'Bell, Book and Candle' – where sinners were eliminated from further entering the faith by a priest who would ring a small bell and slam the Holy Bible shut, often after reading the Malediction. The priest would then extinguish the burning candles. Modern mediums claim to be able to conduct exorcisms without the usual religious trappings by psychically contacting the spirit causing the problems and convincing it to move on to the next spiritual plane of existence. In some cases it is believed that ghosts in need of an exorcism are spirits that have not come to terms with their passing, especially where their demise has been untimely or tragic.

Exorcist is an individual – usually a religious holy man – who is skilled in removing demons from within people or locations.

Extras is a word used to describe faces or whole images of people that mysteriously appear on photographs. There are many reported instances of pictures revealing the image of a long-dead relative, or even someone still alive but living thousands of miles away, when they are developed. In the early days of photography, many of these wispy images were faked, but there are a small number of examples that defy explanation even today.

Fairies are tiny, invisible mythical beings. The pranks they play are sometimes mistaken for the activities of ghosts or poltergeists. Many types of fairies are believed to exist with each one being connected to an element, as in earth (Gnomes), fire (Salamanders), air (Sylphs), and water (Undines), and the colour green is apparently sacred to them. They are said to live in hills, valleys, among the trees and also where there are ancient burial mounds and ancient stone circles.

Family apparition is a ghost that haunts one particular family. When the ghost appears it is an omen that someone in the family is going to die.

Fireball is a Scottish phenomenon. Described as a medium to large sphere, it moves in a smooth and often slow way, most often over stretches of water. Fireballs are thought to be the souls of the departed returning to earth to guide the souls of people who have recently died to the next world.

Galley beggar is an old English ghost referred to as early as 1584 in Reginald Scot's work, *The Discovery of Witchcraft*. This ghost has the appearance of a skeleton and its name is derived from the word 'galley', meaning to frighten or terrify. The classic image is that of a screaming skeleton – head tucked under one arm – encountered on a country road.

Ghosts are different forms of apparitions of deceased human spirits that can appear to any of our five senses. They can be seen as a shadowy human or animal form. They can be heard and may even emit a familiar or offensive odour. They are trapped between worlds.

Ghost buster is a specialist in clearing an area of ghosts, poltergeists, spirits or other haunted activity.

Ghost catcher is a type of wind chime that will clink together as a ghost wisps by.

Ghost hunt describes a conscious effort to search out a known ghost or to visit other places suspected to be haunted.

Ghost-hunter is a person who seeks to find ghosts or haunted places and tries to determine what type of spirit activity is taking place, and why.

Ghost investigation involves going into an area looking for ghosts or hauntings under controlled conditions. Reports are made to document the events. Listing all the reading of the equipment along with time, weather, and temperature as the project unfolds becomes valuable information for the research.

Ghoul is a grotesque, evil spirit with a terrifying face that gains its sustenance by robbing a grave to eat the flesh of the recently deceased. The ghoul was at one time the common word for a ghost in Arabia.

Graveyard ghost is a ghost believed to have special abilities. According to folklore, the first person to be buried in a churchyard was believed to return to guard the site against the Devil. Because this task was so great, a cat or dog was often buried before any human, so it would become the guardian of the dead and remain so until the Crack of Doom.

Gremlins are a recent phenomenon, originating from World War Two in 1939–45 when pilots flying dangerous missions reported seeing strange goblin-like creatures in the aircraft with them. A 'gremlin in the works' is common parlance now for when machinery grinds to a halt.

Grey lady is said to originate from Tudor times. Some say it refers to the ghost of a woman who has been murdered by her lover or one who waits for the return of a loved one. There's another theory that these ghosts represent the Dissolution of the Monasteries, which resulted in the death of many monks and nuns, who would have been dressed in grey habits.

Hallowe'en can be traced back long before the advent of Christianity. Our ancient pagan ancestors celebrated the 'Feast of the Dead' by lighting great bonfires across the country to summon the dead and placate them by offering burnt sacrifices. The Christian Church is thought to have moved the bonfire tradition to 5 November, marking Guy Fawkes's fate, in an attempt to dilute the true meaning of the night. Modern witches still celebrate the night of 31 October by holding feasts and performing magic rituals. According to legend, Satan opens the gates of hell at the stroke of midnight and all spirits of evil are set free to wreak havoc on earth. By cock-crow these spirits must return to hell, where the gates are slammed shut at the first sight of dawn. Any spirit left outside would disintegrate forever.

Haunted chair is an essentially English phenomenon referring to people who have a fondness for a particular armchair coming back as a ghost and being seen in the same chair.

Haunt is the place where the ghost or spirit continues to return. Ghosts usually haunt places and not people.

Haunting is used to describe the repeated display of paranormal activity in a particular area. Some hauntings are thought to be poltergeist energy from a disembodied entity trapped in a certain location or by the energy left behind from a very strong tragic event or accident. Occasionally, hauntings appear to be an intelligent ghost trying to make a connection with someone on the earthly plane to give a message. People can also be haunted, as can any item that may have belonged to someone deceased.

Headless ghosts are the spirits of people whose death occurred because they were beheaded. There is also evidence to suggest that these types of apparitions may be connected to the ancient practice of beheading the corpses of people suspected of being connected in life with witchcraft and sorcery.

Headless horsemen in ghost tradition are believed to be the results of riders who may have been ambushed and decapitated while riding at speed through wooded glades. Another theory is that headless riders are ancient chieftains who lost their heads in battle and still wander the earth in search of their dismembered heads.

Iron is believed to be a sure antidote against all kinds of bad magic and evil spirits.

Lemures is the Roman word given to evil ghosts who return to haunt relatives and friends. Ceremonies to placate these spirits were often held in ancient Rome.

Ley lines are the invisible lines that run between sacred objects or locations.

Luminous body is the faint glow in a dead body to signify a soul's impending departure.

Malevolent entities are angry spirits, often seeking revenge. They sometimes attach themselves to a living being, causing them discomfort and distress. They tend to impose their anger or depressed personality on the human being they possess.

Materialisation is the ability claimed by some mediums to bring into vision a spirit or ghost. One of the first recorded incidents occurred in America in 1860 and was performed by the Fox sisters, founders of modern day spiritualism.

Medium is someone who can communicate with the dead. During a trance state the medium allows the spirit to take over their body so they can deliver a message to the living. The medium does not remember any of this once they come out of the trance. Today the new mediums refer to this as channelling. The big difference is that nowadays the medium remains completely conscious of what he/she says and experiences through the spirit.

NDE (near-death experience) is when a person dies and is revived after a short period of time. The person remembers their death experience and can recall visions of the afterlife, which include ghosts and other paranormal events. Survivors of this experience say it changes their whole outlook on death and they feel as if they can live better lives after this realisation.

Necromancer is a person considered to be a sorcerer or wizard, who has the power to raise the dead and force the spirits to obtain information about the future.

Orbs are globe-shaped lights of energy caught on film, usually during a haunting or other paranormal experience. Orbs are believed to represent the spirit of an individual that has died. They are made up of the energy force that powered their body in life. They may vary in size, colour and density.

Omen is a prediction of a future event.

Oracle is a prophet that can communicate with spirits, ghosts and gods to obtain information.

Ouija Board is a board with cards of numbers – zero to nine – the letters of the alphabet, and the words 'yes', 'no' and 'goodbye' printed on the surface. A glass beaker or wine glass is placed on the table and the consultation can then begin. The board comes with a planchette (a pointer) and once you lightly place your hand on it the pointer will spell out the answers to the questions asked by the players. This 'game' can be dangerous if participants are not fully aware of what they are doing and are not educated in psychic science.

Paranormal is any experience that happens beyond the range of scientific explanation or normal human capabilities, including hauntings, telekinesis, telepathy, clairvoyance, or any other rarity that cannot be justified by the five senses.

Perfumed ghosts manifest themselves in the form of a scent. Many people have experienced smelling the favourite scent of a deceased relative, such as an aunt or grandmother.

Phantom coaches are also known as 'death's messenger', and are apparently seen in silent progress before a death in the family. The horses are always said to be headless and the coaches are described as black and sometimes have the appearance of a hearse. The skeleton-like driver is usually viewed as horrendously ugly, with a fixed grin.

Planchette is a pointer used with an ouija board to communicate with spirits, ghosts, or entities of a higher plane.

Poltergeist is a noisy and sometimes violent spirit. While ghosts haunt and like solitude, poltergeists infest locations and prefer company. The name 'poltergeist' means 'noisy ghost'. Known traits of the poltergeist are banging, thumping, moving objects, levitating, and causing fires. These same results can also be attributed to an unconscious outburst of psychokinesis. More researchers of today feel that much reported poltergeist activity is related to psycho-kinesis rather than a ghost.

Possession is when an evil entity takes over a human body and forces the soul out. This allows the spirit to use the host by exerting its own will. This may totally adjust the host's current personality. Women aged under 20 are most commonly attacked in this way and show clear signs of emotional distress. The discarnate spirit seeks out humans to display emotions of anger, revenge and resentment.

Precognition is the foreknowledge of future events.

Psychic is a person who tunes into phenomena beyond their five senses and has the ability to see or sense the future, present and past. The talents of a psychic include but are not limited to hearing voices, seeing spirits and knowing what might be happening in the future. Unfortunately these gifts have been misinterpreted as mental illness for some. Psychics have also been referred to as seers or sensitives.

Psychokinesis is the ability to move objects using only the power of the mind.

Psychomancy is the ancient art of reading future events through the appearance of ghosts, interpreting what their manifestations to the living might mean.

Purgatory is the place where the souls of the dead must go to be cleansed of all their sins before being allowed into heaven, according to Catholicism.

Reciprocal apparition is an experience where the individual and ghost see and react to one another.

Reincarnation is the belief that once a person dies their soul returns to a new body where it will continue to learn lessons about life and how to reach enlightenment. Many reincarnations may be necessary for the soul to learn and become closer to the goal of perfection.

Retrocognition is the foreknowledge of past events.

Salt, according to ancient customs, is an antidote to all manner of witchcraft and evil spirits. It is said anyone carrying salt in his or her pocket is protected, even against the Devil himself. Placing salt in every corner of rooms in a haunted building is also said to subdue wicked spirits.

Scrying is a form of divination in which an individual stares deeply into an object such as a crystal ball, mirror or flame, in order to see an image that might appear. Such images – usually generated by a spirit – can be symbolic and give answers to a question.

Séance consists of a group of people sitting in a circle holding hands in the hope of contacting the dead. The procedure is conducted by a medium that goes into a trance, as a vehicle for the deceased spirit to take over and communicate with loved ones, sometimes through a spirit guide. Knocking or rapping sounds can also be heard during a séance. The word is of French origin, meaning 'a sitting', and there's no limit to the number of participants, though even numbers apparently get better results.

Sensitive refers to a person who can detect paranormal events beyond the range of their five senses.

Shaman is a medicine man or witch doctor who can communicate with the spirits during a trance and who also possesses the power of healing.

Sixth sense is to have the power of perception in addition to the five senses. It is also a popular term for ESP.

Smudging is a form of cleansing or clearing a spirit from an area by using incense to purify the area.

Spectre is most commonly used now to describe a ghost that is faked or the result of natural factors.

Spirit guide is a heavenly spirit or guardian angel that is present and offers help to the individual to which it is attached. This help may be a simple feeling that comes over the person when they need guidance for a problem or situation. Some people claim they can communicate with their guides at all times.

Spirit photography is usually a photo that contains a face or form believed to be that of a deceased person.

Spiritualism is a belief structure that assumes that spirits and ghosts can communicate with the living.

Supernatural is when an unexplained occurrence take place out of the realm of the known forces of nature. The experience usually involves spirits.

Table-tipping (typology) is a type of communication with the spirit world by using a table. Participants start out with any size table and surround it with a number of people. Everyone places all five fingers lightly on the table. All together the group chants, 'Table up, Table up'. Usually the table will start to quiver or lift to one side. If someone in the group has strong energy the table might rock back and forth or lift off the floor. At this point a question may be asked with a response from the table tapping, once for 'yes' and two for 'no'. If there is a non-believer present the table will probably not move. This type of entertainment can be dangerous and is not recommended to those not skilled in psychic science.

Talisman is a protective charm or amulet said to have the ability to ward off evil.

Telekinesis is where a person can move an object through the power of thought without physical means to move the object.

Telepathy is a method of communication from mind to mind, sometimes across great distances.

Teleportation happens when an object is transported from one location to another by disappearing and then reappearing in a different place.

Time slips occur when the past and present collide at a location.

Trance, a state between being asleep and awake, is where a medium uses his or her body as a channel for waiting spirits to pass messages through to living relatives and friends.

Transmigration is the belief that a soul can move from body to body through the process of reincarnation.

Vassage is a spirit that inhabits a scrying crystal. During a scrying session, the spirit communicates by forming literal or symbolic images.

Vengeful spirits return from the dead to avenge terrible wrongs that have been done to them.

Vortex is a small tornado-shaped image that shows up on pictures when there is a spirit present. Orbs can apparently be seen rotating inside the shaft. Sometimes the vortex is so dense it will cast a shadow. It is believed that the vortex is a means of travel for spirits in the orb form.

Wakes are a noisy ancient custom of watching over the dead while vast amounts of alcohol are consumed. This tradition, especially popular in Ireland, is based on the theory that drinking – as alcohol is a cleanser – helps the spirit of the deceased on its journey to the next world. Music, singing and laughter are encouraged, as it is believed loud noises keep evil spirits at bay.

Warlock is often used to describe a male witch, but this is insulting to many so-called warlocks, as the word has been used in the past to describe a traitor.

White ladies have been seen all over the British Isles, traditionally haunting castles, mansions, halls and even bridges and stretches of water. In ancient times, pagans, to give them a safe passage, apparently sacrificed young women to river gods.

Will-o'-the-Wisp – also known as jack-o-lantern, ignis fatuus, corpse candle and foolish fire – is a ball of flame that floats in mid-air. Such phenomena have also been observed bobbing or dancing just above the ground in yellow and blue flames. These wondrous episodes have been recorded since Roman times. The Native Americans believe them to be a fire spirit warning everyone of danger. The Germans thought the balls of flame were lost or trapped souls that couldn't move on. In Africa some believed that the Will-o'-the-Wisps were witches trying to scare sinners into behaving properly. In Russia, these lights represent the souls of stillborn infants. Throughout Europe when these lights appeared it was thought to be evil spirits that couldn't enter heaven but were not evil enough to be condemned to hell. It would be foolish to follow these strange dancing lights.

Witch is a person – particularly a woman – who practises witchcraft. Most worship nature, but there are different types. Most modern witches would not use their powers for evil, preferring to help human, animal and spiritual awareness. An unwritten law is that witches cannot reveal to anyone what they are or how they practise their art in the belief that silence is power, and power brings knowledge.

Wizard is someone with remarkable abilities and usually proficient in the art of magic. Most male witches prefer this title.

Wraiths are claimed to be the ghost of a person on the edge of death whose appearance should be seen as a warning to the witness that their days are numbered.

PART TWO

THE GHOST
TOUR OF
GREAT BRITAIN

YORKSHIRE

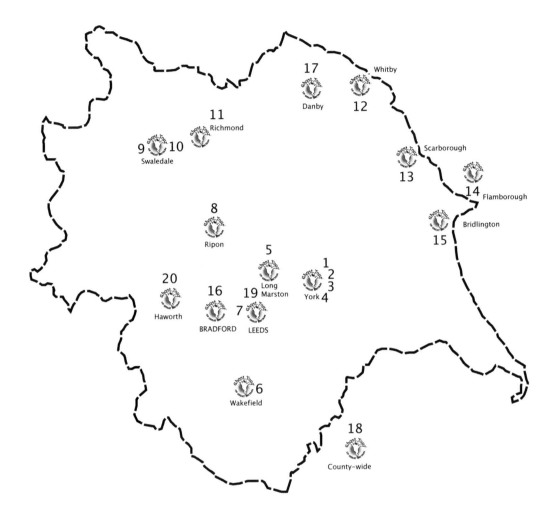

INTRODUCTION

Let him who is a true-born gentleman,
And stands upon the honour of his birth,
If he believe that I have pleaded truth,
From this briar pluck a white rose with me.

William Shakespeare, Henry IV part 1

Once Britain's largest county, Yorkshire defiantly still stands tall, chest puffed out for all its worth, in the north-eastern region of England. Local government administrative changes in the 1970s may have downgraded its status in terms of sheer size, but Yorkshire itself remains as proud as its people, looking down on surrounding counties such as Derbyshire, Lincolnshire, Cumbria and, in particular, red rose neighbours Lancashire.

Anyone born in the white rose county will swear there is no scenery more breathtaking than the scenery of Yorkshire. No moor is quite so atmospheric, no coastline so rugged and no beach more golden.

It would be difficult indeed to find people more proud of their birthplace than Yorkshire men and women. To some, Yorkshire is not only the centre of the universe but a country apart. Locals' claims concerning the uniqueness of this stubbornly northern territory amount, however, to more than mere bluster. Yorkshire's heritage has made it a major attraction for tourists from all parts of the world. The

Yorkshire Dales and North Yorkshire Moors running through its heart are truly stunning and a magnet to visitors.

It is also a county of contrasts. Within its boundaries Yorkshire has an abundance of celebrated and thriving cities such as Sheffield, Bradford, Leeds, Hull and York.

The county's sense of pride and camaraderie is no more evident than in its keen rivalry with Lancashire. The proud inhabitants of Yorkshire once vigorously defended their homeland from incursion by the Lancastrians in a conflict commonly known as the Wars of the Roses. It would be a mistake to assume that the intensity of the rivalry has diminished with time – it prevails still whenever the two counties meet in a cricket match!

It is the build up to the bloody battles between York and Lancaster that Shakespeare is referring to in the lines above. The wars between the white house of York and the red house of Lancaster would eventually decimate the old English nobility.

Since that gory time both roses have been adopted by the English counties of Yorkshire and Lancashire. Factually, however, it should be stressed that the phrase Wars of the Roses was not used until 1829 – coined by Sir Walter Scott in his novel *Anne of Geierstein*.

Yorkshire's diversity ranges from its southern reaches, much of which are industrialised, to relatively unspoiled northern expanses that remain untouched, unblemished farming land.

Down the ages Yorkshire has played host to Vikings, Saxons and of course the invading Romans. Before the Romans arrived, the vast majority of the area now recognised as Yorkshire was in the territory of the Brigantes, an ancient British Celtic tribe that lived between the Tyne and the

Humber valley. Invaders immediately recognised Yorkshire as a highly significant area of Britain.

One of its cities, York, is the ancient capital of Yorkshire, and this 'walled city' was also the nominated capital of both the Vikings and the Romans. Indeed, York is universally regarded as one of the greatest cities of the mediaeval world. York's illustrious history is distinguished by York Minster, one of the finest Gothic churches in the whole of northern Europe. Dominating the city with its vast towers and elegant windows, the Minster oozes historic finery with its shrines, sculptures, beautiful glass and royal monuments.

York has no rival in terms of ancient and historic buildings and it has the most complete circuit of mediaeval city walls anywhere in the country, still with its four main gates intact, complete with ancient heraldry. Visitors are able to walk along the ramparts for almost two miles and take in the spectacular vistas of a city that is a masterpiece of architecture through the ages.

Roman remains are scattered around and the city also boasts one of the only secular Saxon structures to be found in England. While Yorkshire's sporting tradition thrives in the competitive instincts of its people, the county has an artistic soul, characterised by the three Brontë sisters, all of whom were born and raised in the heart of this picturesque and sublimely tranquil county. Novels such as *Jane Eyre* and *Wuthering Heights* ensured Yorkshire would be recognised the world over for the quality of its literature.

Interestingly, the ghost of Emily Brontë has been seen walking on a moorland path near the waterfall at Haworth. On 19 December 1978, the anniversary of her death, she appeared at Weaver's restaurant, where she apparently climbed a staircase that had been removed years before.

Since the mid-1990s I have been leading ghost tours around some of the most haunted places in Britain, and naturally my tour took me north to the remarkable county of Yorkshire, a land rich in legend and folklore, ghosts, entities and black phantom dogs.

Some of the stories you will read here concern real ghosts and spirits. Others are perhaps no more than 'recordings' of past events, traumatic happenings absorbed by Yorkshire's craggy landscape and re-run from time to time, rather like a film that is replayed on a home video or DVD player.

I

TREASURER'S HOUSE, YORK

What better place to start my visit of haunted Yorkshire than in the ancient city of York, where I called in at one of the most haunted country houses in the whole of England. Here I met Ray Alexander, a gentleman who had the foresight to create the original ghost walk in York. He is now part of a team that takes people on ghost tours of the city 365 days a year.

Standing with Ray outside the majestic Treasurer's House, it was easy to get a sense of why this is said to be the most haunted place in York. Situated in the very heart of York Minster, this building, in addition to its ghosts, is renowned as home to one of York's best-loved tearooms!

The first treasurer – responsible for the Minster's silver and other treasures – was appointed in 1091. In addition, the treasurer also acted as host to royal and ecclesiastical visitors.

The original house was burned down in the great fire of York in 1137 and was rebuilt in the reign of Edward I. Although the major part of the house was rebuilt in the 1600s, parts of the original building can be found behind the Jacobean façade.

A confusion of styles makes the interior of the Treasurer's House fascinating, its rooms ranging from chic Georgian to sumptuous Victorian. There is even a Roman influence,

connected to the fact that the house is actually built above Roman remains.

Treasurer's House is so haunted that there is purportedly a ghost story to be told almost in every room.

There is, however, one specific story – inextricably tied to the building's Roman links – that particularly interested me. It happens to be one of the most famous ghost stories in the world as it concerns some of the oldest known ghosts.

Ray Alexander was kind enough to convey the story to me. He explained that the incident occurred in 1953 when an 18-year-old apprentice plumber named Harry Martindale was

working in the cellar at Treasurer's House, fixing pipes. Standing on a small ladder, the young apprentice was getting on with his job when, to his surprise, he heard faintly in the distance the sound of what he thought was a trumpet. The player, however, was no expert. Harry recalled that the noise emanating from another part of the cellar was rather ugly and discordant, similar to that of an old car horn.

The young man did not really think anything more of the sound, but it did strike him as rather unusual that it was able to penetrate all the way down to the cellar of the house.

Returning to his work, in time Harry Martindale paused again from his labours and realised the noise was getting louder… and closer. To the apprentice's bewilderment and horror, a few moments later a Roman soldier appeared, seemingly emerging from a wall directly in front of him, followed by as many as 20 men.

Initially paralysed by fear, Martindale eventually recovered his senses but was so shaken by what he was witnessing that

he fell off his ladder. He picked himself up from the cellar floor and backed away to huddle in a corner of the room. From his crouched position, Harry stared in disbelief as, one by one, soldiers emerged from the wall and strode across the cellar floor in single file as if on a march. They then disappeared through the wall at the opposite end of the cellar.

According to Ray, Harry Martindale was later able to describe his ordeal in great detail. Martindale's main priority, he said later, while in the company of these eerie Roman soldiers, was to stay away from their view. With his brain working overtime, the apprentice reckoned that because he could see the soldiers so clearly, they in turn must have been able to see *him*. Surely it would have taken only one of them to turn his head to the right, see him cowering in the corner and… well, who can tell what would have happened then?

The first thing Martindale noticed about the men was that they seemed to be rather short, probably only chest height if he had been standing up straight. On closer inspection Martindale noticed the troop of soldiers actually appeared to be walking on their knees! He could see nothing at all of calves, ankles and feet.

They were said to be shabbily dressed and not wearing what the apprentice considered 'appropriate' Roman uniform. Their helmets were the only part of a soldier's regalia that matched Martindale's grasp of what he had learned in history lessons at school. He described the troop as fatigued; they gave the appearance of having been on the march for days with little rest.

Another aspect that particularly stuck in Harry Martindale's mind was that one of the soldiers emerged laid out flat on the back of a carthorse. It was impossible to tell, he recalled later, whether the man was asleep or dead.

His ordeal over, Martindale emerged from the cellar and recounted his experience to family and close friends. Subsequently the teenage plumber was asked whether he would 'go public' with his remarkable story and, reluctantly, he agreed to speak to the local press. Soon the sighting of ghostly marching soldiers at Treasurer's House was attracting the attention not only of the people of York, but also the whole country. It was not long before national newspapers, radio stations and television companies were clamouring to interview Harry Martindale.

The young plumber never wavered from his story and told it in exactly the same way to anyone who showed an interest. Despite this consistency of recollection, however, most in the media managed to poke fun at Martindale, rubbishing his improbable story and claiming that the account was no more than the figment of an over-active imagination.

Highly regarded before the incident as a young man of honesty and integrity, Martindale was so hurt and humiliated by the treatment he received at the hands of the media that for many years he refused to speak about his experience in the cellar. Until, that is, years later, when a startling discovery provided the foundation for Martindale to retell his story with renewed confidence.

Ray Alexander explained to me how workmen excavating under Treasurer's House exposed a Roman road. As the excavations continued, it became apparent that 2,000 years earlier the road would have headed out of Roman York and towards the north.

Crucially, in terms of Martindale's story, the road lay 38 centimetres below the cellar floor. So the most confusing – and perhaps comical – element of his account, that he had seen a troop of Roman soldiers marching with no feet, was

finally explained. Because the old Roman road was situated below the cellar floor, Martindale had gained the false impression that the soldiers were somehow walking on their knees!

Treasurer's House is owned and operated by the National Trust and visitors are welcome to come here and enjoy a cup of tea in one of the old cellars. With such a rich paranormal history, Treasurer's House was a fantastic place to start my ghost tour of Yorkshire. It is also an absolute paradise for anybody setting out in search of ghosts.

2

HOLY TRINITY
CHURCH, YORK

The beautiful Holy Trinity Church, just a stone's throw from York Minster, has 12th-century origins. Regarded as York's hidden gem, the Holy Trinity Church took shape in the 13th, 14th and 15th century and is a tranquil, pleasant area; a haven amid the busy streets of York. In the care of the Churches' Conservation Trust, the interior of Holy Trinity has not changed in more than 200 years and, as a result, it is incredibly atmospheric.

This is an amazing place with many stories to tell, but the reason I was at the church was to hear more of the story of a headless ghost. I was fortunate again to have Ray Alexander with me and, as we strolled through to the graveyard, he relayed this strange tale to me.

It starts innocently enough, with a local woman eating her lunch at Holy Trinity Church. Painting a picture of the scene, Ray explained to me that during the summer months the churchyard becomes inundated with people, not only with visitors to York but also with locals seeking a tranquil backdrop during their lunch breaks.

On this particular day the local woman ambled into the churchyard and was surprised to find she was entirely alone; she had the place to herself. This did not unduly trouble the woman, who saw it as an opportunity to claim her favourite bench by the wall. From this vantage point she could see

everything around her. As she started to eat her lunch she looked up and realised she was no longer alone. Also in the churchyard was a man, curiously wearing not ordinary clothes but what looked like a costume. The garb was the type worn probably 450 years before and although she thought it unusual, the woman presumed the visitor was perhaps taking part in a period play in the city or maybe even a film production. Anticipating other actors or crew members would soon follow, the woman kept her watch, but no one else appeared. The only other person in the churchyard was this solitary man, who was pacing restlessly.

On closer inspection, the woman noted that the 'actor' was playing an Elizabethan aristocrat; no expense had been spared on recreating the authenticity of his expensive costume. Although she couldn't see his face, she sensed the man was sad and deeply troubled. He seemed to be walking very slowly with his head bowed as if looking for something on the ground in the churchyard.

Eventually the man disappeared behind the church and the woman turned her attention back to her lunch. However, moments later she sensed once again that she was not alone. Instinctively, she looked up and saw the same man in Elizabethan clothes. He was now walking directly towards her and the grim reality of his 'bowed head' appearance hit home. To her horror she realised what had looked like a bowed head from the rear was, when viewed from the front, no head at all!

As with all good ghost stories, there is a sound explanation for what the woman saw. This ghost is thought to be Thomas Percy, the 7th Earl of Northumberland. Percy lived during the reign of the Protestant Queen Elizabeth I. As a Roman Catholic, Percy was considered a traitor and the punishment for traitors in those days was a barbaric deterrent – a public execution that ended with the victim's decapitation, his head removed and displayed on a wooden pole on one of the city gates.

This was the unfortunate fate of Thomas Percy, who was executed on 22 August 1572. His head was placed on a pole in the city and left there to rot. Two years later, however, Catholic sympathisers removed the head and took it to the Holy Trinity churchyard, where it was buried somewhere within the grounds. The exact location is unknown.

Ray Alexander explained to me that whereas the reclaimed head was buried as part of a religious ceremony, the body, for obvious reasons, was not. Perhaps it is for this reason that the body returns, appearing restless and uneasy as it rises from the place where it was buried. Who knows, maybe it is desperately searching for the place where the head of Thomas Percy now lies?

There is nobody today who can state accurately where Percy's head is buried. Significantly, though, it is said that one particular part of the churchyard occasionally becomes extremely cold and a sense of depression hits the person standing on that spot. Perhaps it is directly beneath this spot in the churchyard that the 7th Earl of Northumberland's head is buried.

Another fascinating ghost story is etched into the history of Holy Trinity Church. This tale dates back to the 1860s and 1870s. The church in the 19th century had a raised gallery, commonplace for this type of establishment during those days. From this vantage point, onlookers could look down along the nave and beyond to the eastern window.

It was from here that members of the congregation often saw three ghostly figures. Unusually, the figures would

always appear in broad daylight and, more often than not, during the morning service. They appeared to be connected to each other, taking the form of a young mother, a child and a maid. The same apparition appeared on each occasion and was witnessed by many people. First the young mother would emerge, seemingly troubled. Next the maid would arrive with the baby in her arms. The three would sit together for a few moments before the mother, kissing her baby first, disappeared, much to the discomfort of the nursemaid and child.

This sequence went on for many years and, once again, there seems to be an explanation for the ghostly sighting. Legend has it that many years ago, a father, mother and baby lived close to Holy Trinity Church. All three died in relatively quick succession, struck down by a plague, but while the father and mother were buried together in York Minster, their young child was buried outside the city's walls. It appears the mother still grieves the separation from her baby and longs for the day when they can be together once more.

Sightings of these three figures, viewed from the raised gallery, became so prominent at one point that onlookers started to believe that what they were seeing must be an illusion created by trees outside the eastern window. As a result, branches were lopped and trees cut down. It seemed to work: for a time the sightings stopped. It proved a brief respite however. Only a few months later, the three figures were seen again at the eastern window, this time during a wedding ceremony at the church.

All went quiet for several years, but then, as recently as 1957, more strange happenings occurred, suggesting that even after all these years the three figures are perhaps still not at rest. Oblivious to this particular aspect of the history

of Holy Trinity Church, a historian and her friend were looking around the grounds. As the historian wandered around the gardens, her friend stood underneath where the raised gallery had once been. Here she experienced what she later described as 'an earthy and cold sensation – an atmosphere of death and decay'. She made a mental note of this, but it was seven years later that she finally researched the story of the three ghostly figures that used to appear at the church's eastern window. Intrigued, she returned to investigate further, but by then all was well in the church. Perhaps the mother, baby and nursemaid have finally found their peace.

3

YORK DUNGEON

When in York, the Dungeon is a tremendous place to visit. Concealed under the paving stones of the city, York Dungeon is now a marvellous museum and appears not too dissimilar to its parent attraction, the great Dungeon in London. Here you can learn of torture, murder, suffering, execution and much more. Revelling in human misery, the Dungeon focuses on more than 2,000 years of suffering.

Modern technology and special effects ensure a frightening experience for any visitor, but there is said to be something altogether more sinister lurking in the bowels of York Dungeon – an actual ghost.

This isn't just any old ghost, however. The Dungeon ghost is said to be that of Yorkshire's most infamous inhabitants, Guy Fawkes, whose effigy is still burned, of course, on every 5 November – Bonfire Night.

Born on 13 April 1570 at Stonegate in Yorkshire, Fawkes is believed to have left England in 1593 or 1594 for Flanders, to enlist in the Spanish army under the Archduke Albert of Austria. He held a post of command when the Spaniards took Calais in 1596 under the orders of King Philip II of Spain and was described at this time as a man 'of excellent good natural parts, very resolute and universally learned'.

Although later depicted as a mercenary ruffian, Fawkes was in fact impressive physically: tall, powerfully built, with thick red hair and a bushy beard. His extraordinary bravery at the Battle of Nieuport in 1600, when it is believed he was wounded, brought him to the attention of the commander of the English Regiment in Flanders, Sir William Stanley. Consequently, in February 1603, Fawkes left the Archduke's forces and headed for Spain on Stanley's behalf to 'enlighten King Philip II concerning the true position of the Romanists in England'. At this time Fawkes and an accomplice named Christopher Wright failed in an attempt to gain Spanish support for an invasion of England on the death of Elizabeth I.

A year later, in May 1604, the gunpowder conspiracy was hatched when Fawkes met with Robert Catesby, Thomas Percy, John Wright and Thomas Wintour at a London inn called the Duck and Drake. The conspirators hired a cellar underneath Parliament in March 1605 and Fawkes assisted in filling the room with barrels of powder, hidden under iron bars and faggots.

Fawkes's undoing was the Monteagle Letter, a vague warning that Catholic peers could become victims of a planned attack on Parliament. This was delivered into the hands of William Parker, 4th Baron Monteagle. Apparently ignorant of the incriminating letter's existence, Fawkes inspected the cellar on Wednesday 30 October, to satisfy himself that the gunpowder was still in place and had not been disturbed. Meanwhile, the leading conspirators met and agreed that the authorities were still oblivious to their actions. Significantly, however, all except Fawkes made plans for a speedy exit from London. Fawkes, with his experience of munitions, agreed to watch the cellar and fire the powder. His orders were to leave for Flanders as soon as the powder was fired, and to spread the news of the explosion on the Continent.

Tipped off by Monteagle, on 4 November, parliamentarians

searched the cellars and discovered Fawkes, together with the gunpowder. Fawkes was arrested and found to be carrying a watch, slow matches and touchwood. Early in the morning of 5 November, the Privy Council met in King James's bedchamber, and Fawkes was brought in, declining to say anything except his name was 'Johnson', a servant of Thomas Percy. In response, the King ordered that Fawkes be tortured. At that time torture was unlawful unless authorised by the King or Privy Council.

The extent of this torture can only be imagined. In all probability he was subjected to the persecution of manacles and the rack and Fawkes's spirit eventually broke. Initially he confessed his real name and, eventually, after several days of relentless torture, those of his fellow plotters. The signature on his confession – a barely legible scrawl – is proof of his suffering.

On the day of the execution of Fawkes and his fellow conspirators, it was reported:

> *Last of all came the great devil of all, Guy Fawkes, alias Johnson, who should have put fire to the powder. His body being weak with the torture and sickness he was scarce able to go up the ladder, yet with much ado, by the help of the hangman, went high enough to break his neck by the fall. He made no speech, but with his crosses and idle ceremonies made his end upon the gallows and the block, to the great joy of all the beholders that the land was ended of so wicked a villainy.*

Why Fawkes should choose now to haunt the county of his birth is a mystery, but his restless soul is said still to wander aimlessly around the dungeons at York to this very day.

4

THE GOLDEN FLEECE, YORK

I met up with Andy Yule, the landlord of the Golden Fleece in York, the city's oldest coaching inn. Mentioned in the York archives as far back as 1503, the Golden Fleece stands directly opposite the city's most historic street, The Shambles, and is said to have five ghosts within its walls. Its haunted status is underlined by its use by the city's Ghost Club for meetings.

Andy told me the story of a Canadian airman who was stationed in and around York during World War Two. The young man was lodging at the Golden Fleece but had been given a few days' compassionate leave as he was experiencing domestic difficulties at home. It was suspected his wife was having an affair.

During the 1940s many Canadian airmen were based in York. They were generally on higher wages than their British counterparts and, when their shifts allowed, could afford to go out 'on the town'.

The airman in this story went out one night and drank too much. Next morning he failed to appear for duty and initially his colleagues assumed he was sleeping off a hangover. It later became obvious, however, that something was wrong, and when a member of staff went to check on him, he was shocked to find his colleague hanging from one of the beams in his room at the Golden Fleece.

Andy told me how a Scottish family regularly visit the Golden Fleece, sometimes as often as three times a year. On a recent sojourn, as the family were resting in one of the rooms, their daughter appeared and asked a curious question: 'What would you do if you saw a ghost, mum?'

The mother's response was one of indifference. Her unconcern soon turned to horror, however, when the young girl pointed across the room in the direction of a ghostly man who appeared to be dressed in full flying gear. The figure seemed to glide across the room before disappearing through a wall at the far end of the room.

That the airman still haunts the place where he died indicates to me he is still unable to rest. Why he returns to the Golden Fleece, I don't know. The Scottish family have recovered from their supernatural experience, and still visit the establishment. The girl, however, still has nightmares.

Gloria Cartwright, whose parents ran the pub after World War Two, apparently slept for eight years in the room next door to the one where the tragic airman died – and she was always too petrified to sleep with the light off.

In recent times an American tourist by the name of April Keenan claimed the ghost touched her as she slept at the pub and, even more bizarrely, it then reappeared at her home in Quincy, California. She apparently woke up one morning to discover she had written, '*Geoff Monroe died The Golden Fleece*' on a piece of paper by her bedside.

Stories of strange happenings at the Golden Fleece do not end with the ghost of the Canadian airman.

The rooms at this historic inn are rather luxurious and guests often take photographs as mementos of their stay. On numerous occasions people who have stayed at the Golden Fleece have posted back photographs showing strange objects that were certainly not in the room when the pictures were taken. Experts have been asked to identify the orb-like objects in these photographs, but none has come up with a satisfactory explanation.

The rear yard is named after Lady Alice Peckett, whose husband, John, was a Lord Mayor of York who owned the Golden Fleece at the turn of the 18th century. Lady Peckett is said to be one of the five resident spirits and several guests have reported seeing her wandering corridors and staircases at the dead of night.

Andy also told me about the little boy who apparently haunts one of the downstairs rooms. He is said to be mischievous and constantly seeks the attention of visitors. What's more, the boy seems to get much amusement from the commotion he causes! Andy himself has witnessed numerous objects, such as salt pots, flying off the table in this room before smashing into a wall.

Such activities suggest to me that this boy could very well be a poltergeist. It is obvious the child enjoys making his presence known, but I was interested to know whether or not Andy had actually seen the ghost. Coincidentally he told me how he had caught sight of the boy, seemingly aged around 11 or 12, for the first time just a week before I spoke to him.

Andy's sighting was supported by a medium from Stranraer, who stayed at the Golden Fleece on a short vacation. The woman told Andy there was so much paranormal activity going on in the place that she could not help getting drawn in by it. As a result she checked out of the Golden Fleece to find a more relaxing venue elsewhere! Before leaving, however, she informed Andy that having made contact with the young boy, she could confirm his name was Tim and that he had been killed in a tragic accident involving a horse and cart. Tim had been trampled to death just by the entrance to the Golden Fleece. Restless, Tim obviously haunts the place to this very day.

5

THE BATTLE OF MARSTON MOOR, LONG MARSTON

When I arrived at Marston Moor, aeroplanes were flying overhead, tractors were out working the fields and it was hard to believe that on 2 July 1644 a huge battle took place on this historic site. A monument now stands in the field, a reminder of that bloody day more than three-and-a-half centuries ago.

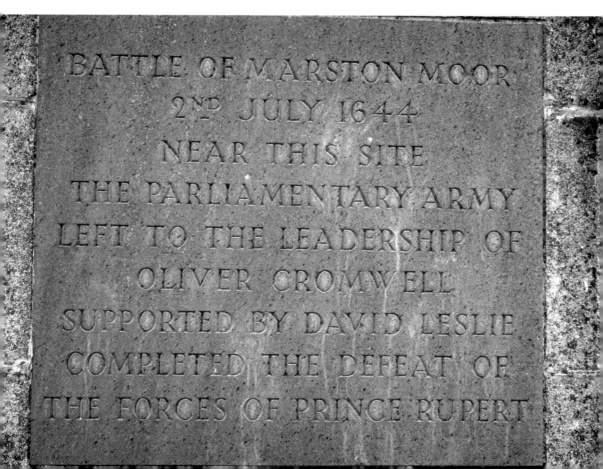

BATTLE OF MARSTON MOOR
2ND JULY 1644
NEAR THIS SITE
THE PARLIAMENTARY ARMY
LEFT TO THE LEADERSHIP OF
OLIVER CROMWELL
SUPPORTED BY DAVID LESLIE
COMPLETED THE DEFEAT OF
THE FORCES OF PRINCE RUPERT

On one side of the field would have stood Royalist commanders Prince Rupert and the Marquis of Newcastle, and, on the other, the allied army of Parliamentary and Scottish forces led by Sir Thomas Fairfax and Lord Manchester, camped out on the hillside now known as Cromwell's Clump.

The Civil War was going poorly for Royalist forces in the north of England and the Marquis of Newcastle was forced to fall back on the fortified city of York. Here Fairfax's Parliamentary armies besieged him.

Prince Rupert's relief force comprised foot soldiers and as many as 7,000 cavalrymen. Getting word of the relief force, Fairfax broke off the siege of York and marched his men south to prevent Rupert from reaching the city walls. In a feat of brilliance, however, Rupert surprised the Parliamentary generals by marching around their defences and making it to York.

Not satisfied with this strategic masterstroke, Rupert now ordered his tired men out from York to surprise the enemy. They met a numerically superior Parliamentary force numbering as many as 27,000 men.

By the time the armies were in position it was late in the day and the headstrong Rupert, convinced his foe would not attack until the morning, left the field in search of his supper. Lord Newcastle was similarly lethargic, retiring to his coach for a quiet smoke.

The resting Royalists were totally stunned by the Parliamentary force's attack, which began as dusk was falling at around 7pm. A full moon shone that night, bringing creepy illumination to the fierce fighting that lasted for several hours. The bloody attack dulled the effectiveness of Rupert's cavalry, and the Parliamentary side's infantry was heroic in victory.

The Royalists lost as many as 3,000 men, plus their artillery train. York was forced to surrender to Parliament and the king effectively lost the north of England.

The 'invincible' Prince Rupert's reputation was now in tatters, but Marston Moor enhanced the growing reputation of Oliver Cromwell.

On the monument at the battle site is this inscription:

Battle of Marston Moor 2nd July 1644. Near this site, the Parliamentary Army, left to the leadership of Oliver Cromwell, completed the defeat of the forces of Prince Rupert.

Rupert's men are buried in huge, unmarked graves in the fields of Marston Moor and on rare occasions people say they have seen the battle being refought as the sun sets here. Phantom soldiers can be seen walking about the moor and the sounds of guns and cannon can be heard.

A specific example of this occurred one evening in 1968. A

group of tourists were lost along the A59 road running through Marston Moor. They were searching for the road leading to Hessay, and as they carried on down a lane, they saw to their surprise a group of people in fancy dress – or so they thought. In full view of the tourists were bedraggled soldiers wearing an expression of weariness and disillusionment.

Not wishing to get involved with this strange ensemble, the tourists carried on down the road before turning back to glance one last time at the peculiarly dressed men. Imagine their surprise when they saw only a lonely road – the soldiers had completely disappeared.

Somewhat perturbed, the tourists reported their experience and were informed about the ancient battle. It was only then that they realised what they had witnessed was not men in fancy dress at all, but a group of ancient soldiers.

This wasn't an isolated sighting however. Five years later on the same road, two tourists were walking along when they witnessed the same event, just yards from Marston Moor, where the battle took place all those years ago. My theory is that the soldiers seen by these people are not ghosts at all but images from a natural recording of the Battle of Marston Moor. It is all to do with tragic, traumatic and premature death. Murders, suicides and battles have all the ingredients for an event that records itself into the very fabric of the place where it happens. Soldiers who died years before their time at Marston Moor could have created energy in resisting death that ensures the scene was recorded into the soil of the moor. When atmospheric conditions are right, the scene is replayed. So the battle is played out over and over again, just like a favourite old film being watched regularly on a home video player.

HERE IN HIS NATIVE COUNTY
SIR THOMAS FAIRFAX
THE FAMOUS YORKSHIRE SOLDIER
FOUGHT FOR PARLIAMENT
WITH BRILLIANCE AND SUCCESS
LORD GENERAL OF
THE PARLIAMENTARY ARMY
— 1645 – 50 —

I really do not believe that the people who still see ancient soldiers on Marston Moor are seeing ghosts. What they witness are simply recordings of a very tragic event that took place on the moor on that summer's evening in 1644.

It is interesting to note that Marston Moor is not the only place to have witnessed ghostly activities in relation to the battle between the Royalist and Parliamentary forces. The Old Hall at the village of Long Marston, one mile north of the battle site, is also said to be haunted. Cromwell used the hall as a base before the battle took place and it is his ghost that is said to appear in the hall.

6

WAKEFIELD

The West Yorkshire town of Wakefield has its own ghostly accounts. Mary Bolles of Heath Hall left a curious instruction in her will – she stated the room in which she died was to be permanently sealed.

When death came to Mary in 1661, the executors of her will carried out her wishes and the room was accordingly closed off.

Fifty years later, however, it was reopened, and after this the ghost of Mary Bolles never ceased to haunt the hall. In an attempt to calm her restless spirit, stone effigies were laid on Mary's tomb in Ledsham Church, but to no avail.

A caretaker at the hall reported that his Alsatian guard dog would refuse to go anywhere near the death room and soldiers stationed at Heath Hall during World War Two claimed to have seen the ghost.

Although the house has now been demolished, the door of the haunted bedroom is preserved for posterity in Wakefield Museum.

Wakefield also boasts a ghost that has a connection with a modern-day phenomenon – a multi-screen cinema. An unwelcome special guest star – a ghostly image that wanders around the 12 viewing rooms – has disrupted screenings at Cineworld Cinemas in the town. The apparition has been witnessed by staff members and spooked customers.

7

THE VESPER GATE, KIRKSTALL

My ghost tour of Yorkshire led me to Kirkstall Abbey, which dates back to 1152. Here a former abbot is said to haunt an area that has been converted into a museum. Local tradition suggests it is more usual to hear the spirit moving around than to actually see him.

Photo: D. Redfern

Perhaps it is the ghost of Abbot John Ripley, who retired to live in the gatehouse – the oldest part of the building. In the 19th century a stone coffin containing a skeleton, thought by some to have been that of Abbot Ripley – was discovered under the floor of the abbey's Norman Hall.

Equally fascinating though was my visit to a pub, a stone's throw from the abbey across the A65 road. It is called the Vesper Gate and I was intrigued to learn, by chance, that this pub is haunted.

The Vesper Gate is a traditional, attractive pub and a great place to go for a pint… and to hear a ghost story.

The pub is said to accommodate the ghost of an elderly man in a flat cap who wanders around the bar area.

I spoke to one of the regulars at the Vesper Gate and he confirmed that, although he had not actually seen the ghost, he had on numerous occasions been in the bar when ashtrays had shattered on the tables for no apparent reason. He told me that rather than the ashtrays flying off the table and smashing into a wall, a phenomenon commonplace in haunted pubs, at the Vesper Gate they simply explode on the table!

I inspected the pub's ashtrays and discovered they were not flimsy, plastic objects. Large and made from sturdy glass, these ashtrays should certainly not smash of their own accord. I was convinced at the end of my visit to the Vesper Gate that the ghostly activities here bore all the hallmarks of an active poltergeist.

Photo: D. Redfern

8

FOUNTAINS ABBEY, NEAR RIPON

Lying four miles west of Ripon in North Yorkshire is Britain's largest monastic ruin, Fountains Abbey. Situated on a

beautifully preserved and historic estate, the abbey was founded in 1132 by 13 Benedictine monks seeking a simpler life. Fountains Abbey attracts an incredible 300,000 visitors a year and is now in the hands of the National Trust. It became a World Heritage Site in 1987.

Monks inhabited the abbey from 1132 until 1539 when, through Henry VIII's Dissolution of the Monasteries order,

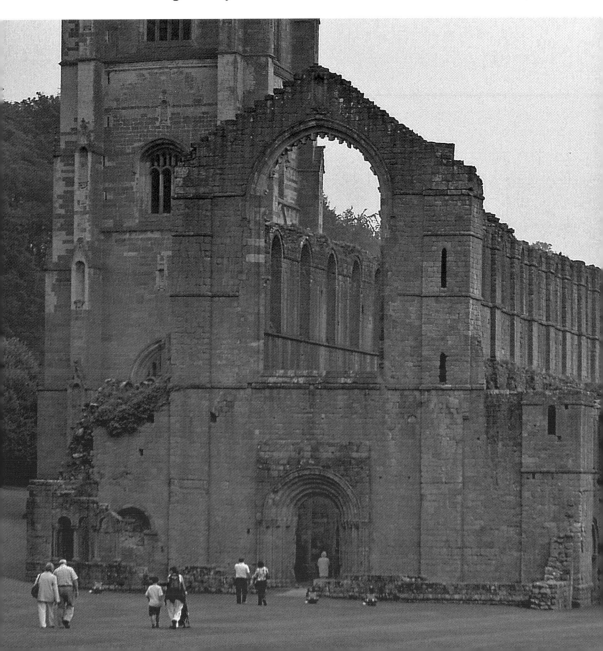

they were forced out of the estate. The Crown then sold the abbey buildings and more than 500 acres of land to Sir Richard Gresham, a merchant. The property was passed down through several generations of Sir Richard's family, finally being sold to Stephen Proctor, who built Fountains Hall at the turn of the 17th century. Stone from the abbey ruins was used in the construction of the hall.

A blue ghost is said to reside in Fountains Hall. Legend suggests it is that of Stephen Proctor's daughter, who witnessed her father's evil doings and remains at the hall for eternity. An Elizabethan man has also been seen emerging from the panelling in a stone hall.

Walking around the grounds, it is easy to imagine the pain and suffering that must have taken place when Henry VIII ordered the closure of Fountains Abbey. I certainly sensed the disquiet around the building.

On certain occasions, it is said, when all is silent and still, the distinctive sound of a phantom choir of monks can be heard, their chanting emanating from the abbey's Chapel of Nine Altars. Perhaps the sound of the monks' singing is an indication that, despite having left their home physically all those years ago, spiritually the monks will always remain at the old Cistercian abbey, and their presence will never be diminished.

9

THE PUNCH BOWL INN AND THE CORPSE WAY, SWALEDALE

I visited the haunted Punch Bowl Inn at Swaledale on the North Yorkshire moors, an historic pub where mourners would have come hundreds of years ago as they made the daunting journey to bury their loved ones at the aptly named Grimston Church.

There is a 12-mile road stretching all the way to Grimston Church. It is known as the 'Coffin Road', or 'Corpse Way'. Anybody who died within a 12-mile radius of this area had

to be brought to the church to be buried in consecrated ground.

Before the funeral procession set out, usually from the home of the deceased, all the guests, family and friends would arrive at the house where biscuits and ale would be distributed ahead of the trek. And what a journey it was. It could take up to two days to get to the church. The coffin would have to be carried and the mourners would take it in turns along the Corpse Way's extended, slow crossing through the valley.

It was an arduous passage and the mourners would stop for rests at convenient points, looking out in particular for various stones and places along the way where the coffin could be stored.

One such stone, known as 'The Coffin Stone', is aptly named as it is indeed in the shape of a coffin.

This place is haunted not by a human ghost, but by a large black dog with red staring eyes, huge feet and fangs. It has been seen leaping over the parapet of a bridge on the Corpse Way, but, strangely, there is never a splash when it hits the water.

The funeral cortège would continue along the valley and stop for the night in the little hamlet of Blades, a little way up the hill from the Punch Bowl Inn. Here the body would be stored in what was eerily named 'the Dead House'. Family and friends would go down to the Punch Bowl for the wake before returning up the hill to sleep the night. They would then continue their journey with the coffin to the church where the deceased person would finally be laid to rest.

I was not just here to take in the impressive history of the pub, however. I was interested in the ghost that is said to haunt it. I spoke to Lorraine, the landlady at the Punch Bowl

Inn, and she told me about a doctor who used to regularly drink in the pub during the 1970s. When he died he was buried in the cemetery next door to the pub. Clutching a bottle of port, his favourite drink, the doctor's ghost is sometimes seen walking through the Long Room, one of the rooms

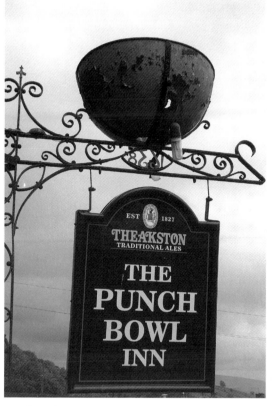

Photo: S. Lilley

in the pub. Significantly, the gregarious doctor was even buried with a bottle of port and it is probably this same bottle that he holds when visitors to the Punch Bowl Inn see his ghost.

Other paranormal happenings have also been reported at the pub, including strange noises and lights switching themselves on of their own accord. Dogs that live in the pub are said to bark frequently as if they sense an intruder despite the fact that nobody else is around. The dogs are said to stop and stare as if something else is in the room with them, almost like they can see something we can't.

10
THE DEAD HOUSE AND
BEYOND, SWALEDALE

Just up the road from the Punch Bowl Inn on the North Yorkshire moors I eventually found the Dead House. It took me about half a day to find what I was looking for – but it was well worth the wait. On a spine-chilling, damp and dark day, I finally approached a place so appropriately named, seemingly situated in the middle of nowhere. There was a strange feeling of unease around the place. Who can tell how

Photo: S. Lilley

many bodies have been stored in this building, which dates from mediaeval times?

I don't know of any specific ghost stories regarding the Dead House but just being in the place and getting a sense of the atmosphere was ghostly enough for me. If I was out on the moors in a storm and this was the only building to shelter in, there is still no way I would even contemplate staying the night in the Dead House.

Continuing down past the Dead House, I walked along the original Coffin Road. The mourners would have walked along this same pathway to the wake.

Carrying on down, I walked across the haunted bridge where the ghostly figure of a red eyed, black dog has, on rare occasions, been seen to leap over the bridge without making so much as a splash. However, for reasons unknown, the dog has not now been seen for over 100 years.

Photo: D. Redfern

Eventually I reached the journey's end, where the mourners would lay down the coffin for the last time as they reached the church at Grimston.

The church itself has many ghost stories, one of which concerns a lead miner. Until the 1600s, people could be buried in linen clothes. However the government of the day introduced a law stating that all deceased people must be buried in woollen clothes. Interestingly, this legislation was designed to help the ailing woollen industry in the country!

This created a predicament for our lead miner, whose daughter's dying wish was to be buried in a linen dress. For flouting the law of the land, the lead miner was fined £5, a huge amount of money in those days. The disgruntled, grieving father is said to still haunt the churchyard to this very day.

I I
THE DRUMMER BOY'S
STONE, RICHMOND

I visited Richmond in North Yorkshire, and with its sense of history, cobbled streets, Georgian architecture and its stunning abbey and monuments, it is not too hard to see why this town has a few ghost stories to tell.

In front of me was Richmond Castle, built in 1071 by Alan the Red, a kinsman of William the Conqueror. The castle's original purpose was to protect Swaledale and its inhabitants against potential border raids.

Although little remains of the original construction, Richmond Castle can be rivalled only by Colchester and Durham as the oldest stone-built castle in England.

A famous ghost story is connected with the castle and involves a mysterious underground passage, which is said to connect the castle to nearby Easby Abbey, a house of the Premonstratensians that was founded around 1152.

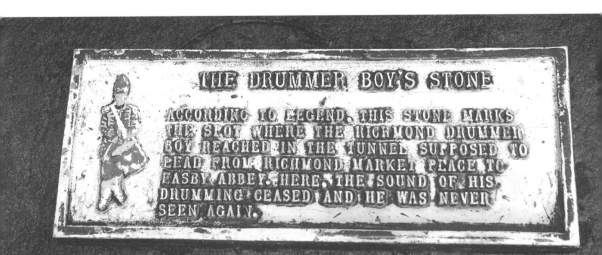

To find out more about the story, I made my way to a small stone monument called 'The drummer boy's stone'.

The plaque on the stone reads:

According to legend, this stone marks the spot where the Richmond drummer boy reached in the tunnel, supposed to lead from Richmond market place to Easby Abbey. Here the sound of his drumming ceased and he was never seen again.

During the latter part of the 18th century a group of Yorkshire militia were stationed at Richmond Castle. Underneath the castle keep, a tunnel was discovered which, it was decided, should be explored. As the entrance was too small for a fully-grown soldier to get through, it was decided to send one of the young drummer boys down the tunnel instead. The boy was told to take his drum to beat as a signal to those listening above, who would trace the route of the tunnel by following the sound. As he marched along the tunnel the boy maintained a steady beat and the soldiers followed the sound of the drumming from above, all the way to the centre of Richmond. Still the drumming continued, as the tunnel somehow ran underneath the River Swale. When they reached the point where the memorial stone is now erected, about half way between the castle and Easby Abbey, the drumming stopped. The soldiers returned to the tunnel entrance and waited – but the drummer boy failed to return and was never seen again.

The stone was erected to commemorate the bravery of the young drummer and some say it is here, on the anniversary of the event, or on a dark and still winter's night, that the faint sound of a ghostly drumbeat pierces the air.

12
WHITBY

Situated 20 miles north of Scarborough, Whitby is a popular fishing town with many claims to fame. Tourists visit in vast numbers, making it a thriving holiday resort, and Whitby has been home to many celebrated people down the years, including the famous 18th-century explorer Captain James Cook.

When I visited Whitby it was a dark, wet and windy day. The weather made the place all the more atmospheric and

Photo: D. Redfern

mysterious, which seemed rather appropriate, as Whitby is known as a ghost-hunter's paradise.

Whitby owes its origins to a famous abbey that has connections with the literary world's most frightening ghoul, Count Dracula. The abbey was founded here in 657 by Oswy, King of Northumberland, to redeem a vow that if God would grant him victory over his rival Penda, the Pagan king of Mercia, he would build a monastery, and consecrate his daughter, Ethelfleda, then scarcely one year old, to the services of God by a life of celibacy. The prayers of Oswy were heard; Penda was slain with most of his nobles and Oswy in gratitude built the monastery of Streanshalh, for monks and nuns of the Benedictine order. He appointed Lady Hilda, niece of Edwin, the first Christian king of Northumbria, abbess. This lady was so famous for her sanctity that she attained the name of St Hilda, and the monastery, though dedicated to St Peter, is generally called after her.

The story goes that in her time, Whitby was terribly overrun with serpents, but these, by the prayers of St Hilda, were decapitated and turned into stones!

Supporting this legend, ammonitae or snake-stones are found in almost every place where alum-rock exists, and particularly in Whitby Scarr, between the high and low water mark. The snakes are all enclosed in hard elliptical stones and in every way resemble the reptile in their form and shape, except for the head, which is always missing.

St Hilda's ghost is regarded as the most famous in Whitby. She is said to be buried somewhere close to the abbey and locals believe she can be seen in summer and winter, standing in the top window at Whitby Abbey, dressed in a shroud.

The most tragic ghost at the abbey is probably that of a

nun, Constance de Beverly, who was determined to break her sacred vows for the love of a brave but false knight called Marmion. To prevent the marriage, Constance was taken to one of the cells at the abbey and bricked up. Her lonely ghost is said to wander around Whitby Abbey to this day, begging for her release.

Invading Danes destroyed the monastery in 867, and it lay in ruins until the Norman Conquest, when Whitby was assigned to Hugh de Abrincis and then William de Percy. The latter refounded the monastery and dedicated it to St Peter and St Hilda. The abbey shared the fate of other monastic establishments during the reign of Henry VIII.

Adding to the creepiness of this ancient ruin is its situation. Unlike the other great religious houses in this country, which were generally built in warm, sheltered situations, Whitby Abbey stands in a bleak spot at least 240 feet above the sea. Its prospect is commanding, high above the town and port of Whitby. Rising on the horizon in front are the frowning heights of the black moors, while to the rear is the vast expanse of the ocean.

In relatively modern times, the abbey was shaken to its foundations by an awesome storm on the night of 2 December 1763, when the whole western wing – though supported by at least 20 strong Gothic pillars and arches – was brought to the ground.

No wonder then that the haunting remains of Whitby Abbey inspired portions of Bram Stoker's *Dracula*.

The graveyard situated next to the abbey overlooks Whitby Harbour and this is the same harbour in which Dracula's ship lands on the shores of England in the midst of a powerful storm.

Named St Mary's Churchyard, it is here that Lucy meets

Dracula – and the place is just as spooky and mysterious in real life.

Away from the monastery, Whitby boasts natural curiosities, not least the various petrifactions found in the alum-rocks. The petrified shells of sea-fish have been found in the cliff on the east side of the mouth of the Eske. Much more sinister though was the discovery by a Dr Woodward, in the early part of the 18th century, of the petrified arm and hand of a man, in which all the bones and joints were perfectly visible!

In 1743, the Revd Mr Borwick found in the alum-rock the complete skeleton or petrified bones of a man. He sent his find to a museum.

An unexplained phenomenon was unearthed in 1758 when the petrified bones of a crocodile, an animal never previously recorded in this part of the world, were taken out of the rock and sent to the Royal Society.

Among the many spirits and entities in Whitby is the ghost of a man called Hob, who is said to leap out in the middle of the road, causing motorists to swerve. Mischievously, he is known also to turn signposts around, causing chaos throughout the town.

There have also been numerous sightings of a ghost who goes by the name of Goosey. His name derives from the fact that he took on a bet to eat a whole goose in one session. For some reason he was later murdered. Whether or not his murder had anything to do with the bet, nobody knows.

There is also a coach and four that can be seen at certain times. Thundering along Green Lane, it heads to the top of the hill and plunges over the cliffs, down into the sea. Perhaps this is a recording of a past accident that occurred on Green Lane many years ago.

13

SCARBOROUGH

CASTLE

Situated grandly on the edge of a cliff along the North Yorkshire coast, Scarborough Castle is the dominant feature for miles around. Three hundred feet below is the town of Scarborough and its harbour. The look of this seaside town has changed substantially down the years, but the castle has been a constant factor since the early part of the 12th century. Indeed, the headland of Castle Hill has been occupied for more than 2,500 years.

Remains of the early stone fortress, built by William le Gros, include a chapel and the curtain walls that were fortified by Henry II in the second part of the 12th century. Henry II was also responsible for replacing the original gate tower with a more sophisticated three-storey keep. This in turn was protected further by a traditional forebuilding.

The top of the keep has disappeared down the centuries, but the lingering walls provide a good indication of how impressive this structure once was. Fireplaces at the first and second levels can still be seen in the walls. Only the foundations remain of the once prodigious forebuilding.

Successive kings and queens after the reign of Henry II regarded Scarborough Castle as a vital strategic defence, and further improvements and additions made the structure virtually impregnable. The barbican, much altered in later

years, was completed in the 14th century, providing extra defence to the castle grounds. Its two half-cylindrical towers were sited either side of a gateway and the approach was protected by two further towers located on a flanking wall.

On only two occasions in 900 years of proud defence of the realm has Scarborough Castle sustained serious damage. It was subjected to prolonged cannon fire during the English Civil War in the 17th century, and in 1914 many of the remaining structures were destroyed by German battle cruisers.

With such a long history, it is unsurprising to discover that Scarborough Castle has an abundance of supernatural activity and ghosts. One such ghost is that of Piers Gaveston, a personal favourite and life-long friend of King Edward II, who reigned from 1307–28.

Both his people and his own father (Edward I) thought Edward incompetent and frivolous. He was thought to be largely under the influence of his favourites, especially the Gascon squire Gaveston – widely believed to be the king's lover. Because he was not as astute in military matters as his father, Edward II lost many of the strongholds taken by Edward I during his campaigns.

The barons became more disgruntled and in 1312 seized Gaveston at Scarborough Castle, executing him at Kenilworth. Edward II's wife Isabella, the daughter of Philip IV of France, left Edward and took their son, the future Edward III, to France. She returned in 1326 to depose and murder Edward.

Before he left Scarborough Castle, Gaveston was promised a fair trial – but the barons reneged on this agreement. He was tried in haste in the Great Hall at Warwick before being taken away to be beheaded.

The ghost of Piers Gaveston has been seen on frequent occasions, staring out forlornly from one of the open windows of Scarborough Castle. Legend has it that he has even attempted to lure people over the cliffs to their deaths. Why does Gaveston haunt Scarborough Castle when he was killed near Warwick? Nobody knows. Perhaps it is just that a ghost who seems to fit Gaveston's description haunts the castle, or, more likely, perhaps it is because it is here that he was assured and promised a safe conduct but did not get it. There are many more ghostly happenings at the castle. At the centre of one haunting is an ancient Roman signal station. I was told about a photograph that was taken by one of the English Heritage staff at Scarborough Castle. On the image is a strange, white, glowing orb, clearly visible as it floats above the old Roman stone walls.

An interesting new theory concerning orbs has arisen among experts in the paranormal. Some now believe these could be the first manifestation of a ghost. Inexperienced ghost-hunters traditionally expect apparitions to take on the appearance of a monk or headless body, but it is a growing conviction that these strange orange and white orbs seen in so many places could, in fact, be ghosts.

The resort of Scarborough also has a 'Pink Lady', one Lydia Bell, who apparently haunts the street where she was murdered in 1804. It is said too that a black horse has haunted Scarborough since Norman times, appearing out of a thundercloud.

14
THE TWO BROTHERS, NORTH LANDING, FLAMBOROUGH

North Landing in Flamborough, East Yorkshire, is famous for its smugglers' caves and panoramic views north along the coast to Filey and Scarborough. It was once the focal point of Flamborough's small but active fishing industry, and even today a few cobles – the distinctive local fishing boats – can still be seen.

It was here in 1927 that a young boy by the name of Tom Gaunt arrived from Scarborough with his father on a sketching expedition. From a cave Tom took a photograph of the empty cove with his little camera. Curiously, when his photographs were developed, he noticed on the print the figures of two men. Neither had been in the cove when he took the photograph. This naturally perplexed young Tom, but history has a very simple way of explaining why the two ghostly figures appeared on the photograph.

In 1909, when fishing was far less advanced and more hazardous, a vessel called *The Gleaner* was out fishing during a violent winter storm. The boat was hit by a large wave and tipped over. Valiantly, another boat called *The Two Brothers* came to the rescue of the four men on board *The Gleaner* and, after successfully picking them up, started heading for the safety of land.

Unfortunately, conditions worsened and the storm grew ever more aggressive. *The Two Brothers* was soon in great difficulty and, in similar fashion to *The Gleaner*, the small boat overturned with the loss of all six men on board. The drowned bodies of four of the men were recovered and buried in the local churchyard, but two of the crew – Robert Cross and Melichay Chadwick – were never found.

It is believed that Tom Gaunt's photograph, taken 18 years after the tragedy, shows the ghosts of two tragic seamen who still haunt North Landing to this day. Perhaps the reason they are so restless is because they never received a Christian burial in consecrated ground, unlike the four other victims of *The Two Brothers* who, so far as we can tell, now rest peacefully.

The ghost of a young girl called Jenny Gallows is also said to haunt this same spot at Flamborough. According to local tradition, if children's games disturb Jenny's ghost, it can be made to disappear by the chanting of a rhyme.

The ghost of a headless woman has also been reported in the area and an ethereal 'White Lady' is said to haunt Danes' Dyke, an Iron Age earthwork nearby.

15
BURTON AGNES HALL,
NEAR BRIDLINGTON

Situated on the north-east coast of Yorkshire, six miles from Bridlington, Burton Agnes Hall is a beautiful Elizabethan building with a grand history dating back to Norman times. Now under the guardianship of English Heritage, the hall has spent much of its illustrious past playing host to establishment families. Despite its apparent charming and

Photo: D. Redfern

welcoming façade, however, it is not necessarily as peaceful as it appears.

Roger de Stuteville built the original Norman manor house in 1173 and the lower chamber still survives in all its gloomy splendour. One of de Stuteville's daughters was named Agnes and she may have been responsible for the name of Burton Agnes.

The upper room of the ruin, constructed in the mid-15th century, is thought to have been the Great Hall of Sir Walter Griffith.

The current house was built when, in 1599, Sir Henry Griffith was appointed to the Council of the North, based in York. Although he had already started to build a new home in the Midlands, this was abandoned in favour of the more strategically positioned site at Burton Agnes. The architect was Robert Smithson, Master Mason to Elizabeth I and builder of other famous houses such as Longleat, Wollaton and Hardwick.

Photo: D. Redfern

Above the entrance of this magnificent red-brick construction is the date 1601, with the initials of Sir Henry Griffith and his wife. Inside, another date – 1610 – is carved into the frieze of the south-east bedroom. The building would have been practically finished by then and 1610 was also the date of the Gatehouse.

It is the ghost of a member of the Griffith family that took me to Burton Agnes Hall. Catherine Anne Griffith, the daughter of Sir Henry, took a great interest in the construction of the building of the house and, when it was completed, proclaimed it to be one of the most beautiful houses in the whole of England. She was sublimely happy and lived at the hall with her family.

Early in 1620, while visiting family friends about a mile from the hall, Catherine Anne was attacked near St John's Well by a robber. Badly beaten, she was found lying unconscious in a pool of blood. She was taken back to Burton

Photo: S. Lilley

Agnes Hall and lingered for a few days, in immense pain and quite delirious, before passing away at the home she loved so much.

She made a dying wish to her sister, requesting that a part of her should forever remain within the walls of her beloved home. The request was not for the squeamish, for she asked that her head be cut off and kept in the house! Unsurprisingly, her wish was ignored and she was buried in the adjoining churchyard.

Within days of the funeral service her ghost started to walk in the house and caused much unrest among the family. The wailing and restless figure of Catherine Anne Griffith became so frequent that the family brought in exorcists who recommended that the body be exhumed. The Griffith family followed this advice and the coffin was opened. As Catherine Anne was not long dead, her body was still intact... but to the family's bewilderment they saw that the head had lost all its flesh and was already just a skull.

Belatedly carrying out Catherine Anne's final wish, the Griffith family had the head cut off and brought back into the house. For many years it had pride of place in the Great Hall and the spirit of Catherine Anne seemed to be at peace.

In time, however, staff working in the Great Hall became understandably spooked by this strange memento on the mantelpiece and one day it was thrown out by one of the servants and placed in the old Norman manor house close by.

It didn't take long before the homesick skull began to scream. Poltergeist activity became prominent again in the hall and the family decided the best thing was to have the skull reburied. Predictably, whenever the skull of Catherine Anne Griffith was reburied, her ghost walked once more.

Finally, the decision was taken to ensure her spirit could be at rest once and for all – by walling up the skull somewhere inside the hall. To this day, no one knows the exact location of Catherine Anne Griffith's skull, but perhaps because she no longer has a 'room with a view', paranormal activity is still recorded at Burton Agnes Hall. Footsteps are heard on landings and an icy atmosphere takes over some of the rooms from time to time.

I spoke to a gentleman who had worked at the hall for 59 years and, although a disbeliever himself, he told me of the many stories he had heard of strange happenings, especially the sound of footsteps walking up and down the stairs on the bottom floor. Problems have been experienced too with a burglar alarm after its sensors – at the bottom of the staircase – regularly detected movement when no one was there. Despite everything being still, the burglar alarm would be randomly set off, as if somebody or something was there. The gentleman then suggested installing a different sort of alarm, one that sensed heat rather than movement. It was a clever idea. Ghosts are not generally associated with heat and since the installation of a new intruder system, the ghost of Catherine Anne Griffith has never been known to trigger the alarms at Burton Agnes Hall.

16

BOLLING HALL,
BRADFORD

Being an historian as well as a ghost-hunter, it's very exciting for me when I find a ghost story that is well documented and goes back for hundreds of years. You get so many tales these days of landlords, shop keepers and hoteliers taking over premises and suddenly they become haunted. I'm not saying that they're not, because some people are more sensitve than others, and although someone can occupy a property for 30 years and never see a ghost, and then say the place is not haunted, someone else can come along and a fortnight later his wife has seen a ghost in one of the bedrooms. Purely and simply because she is more sensitive and has a gift.

I like to go into the history of a place and find newspaper reports, first-hand evidence accounts and possibly an entry in history books. So you can imagine how excited I was when I went to visit Bradford's most haunted house, Bolling Hall, which has something like 20 different sightings of ghosts. Just like Temple Newsam in Leeds, the building is now a museum and has been run by Bradford Corporation since 1912. It is, of course, open to the public. The first known reference to the Manor at Bolling occures in the Domesday Book in 1086 when it was held by Ilbert De Laci. How long the De Laci family held Bolling is not known, but by 1316 a William Bolling had become Lord of the Manor. The Hall passed to the Tempest family in 1497. At the beginning of the Civil War, Richard Tempest fought for the King, and Bolling Hall became the Royalists' headquarters for the siege of Bradford in 1643. The Royalist commander was the Earl of Newcastle and he stayed at the Hall. Before the siege took place, a preliminary skirmish occurred in which the leader of one of his squadrons of horse, the Earl of Newport, was killed. Separated from his men and captured, Newport asked the Puritan leader for quarter. He replied that the Earl would indeed receive quarter, 'Bradford quarter', and immediately struck him a fatal blow with his sword. Because of this Newcastle swore that he would avenge the Earl's death and gave orders to kill everyone in the town, men, women and children, and to give them all 'Bradford quarter' for his friend the Earl of Newport's sake. After giving these orders the Earl went to bed. During the night he was woken by the apparition of a woman who pulled back his bedclothes and then started wringing her hands and wailing, 'Pity poor Bradford'. The Earl was terrified by the apparition. With the dawning of a new day, the Earl countermanded his savage orders and told his men only to kill those who offered armed resistance during the fighting. As a result only 10 people were recorded killed. This incident was recorded at the time by Joseph Lister, who was only 16 and printed the story in a broadsheet dated 1643. This is the earliest recorded sighting of a ghost at the Hall.

One of the most famous Derbyshire ghost stories is that of the Screaming Skull at Tunstead Farm. Dicky O' Tunstead was a soldier. When he returned home from the wars, legend has it that he was murdered by his cousin. Any time anyone tried to bury his skull it began to scream and bad things would happen at the farm. It became so famous that a postcard was made with a picture of the skull on it. That's all I knew until I went to Bolling Hall and was shown the haunted bed. This was sent from Tunstead to Offerton Hall in Derbyshire in 1877. Antique beds were often passed on as family heirlooms. In 1912 the bed came to Bolling Hall. In the head of the bed I was told there is a recess where Dicky is reputed to have kept his money. The story I was also told was that he was a wealthy miser. One night robbers broke into Tunstead Farm and battered him to death and took his money. Family members at Offerton Hall in the 19th century claimed to see his head in the recess when the moon shone directly on it. The same story was also reported after the bed came to Bolling Hall.

After 1816 the Hall was tenanted by a number of families. In the 1840s William Walker and his family lived in part of the Hall. A friend of the family, Richard Oastler, was visiting the Hall and was talking to Mr Walker's eldest son, who told him he did not believe in an afterlife. Oastler told him to repent or he would haunt him himself. On 22 August 1861, Walker's son woke up to see Mr Oastler standing over his bed. He later stated in an interview with the Bradford *Telegraph and Argus*:

> *There with his back turned and long white hair hanging over stooping shoulders was Richard Oastler. I was startled, certainly. But I had no sense of fear. I rubbed my eyes and made sure I was awake, but still the ghost (if that is what it was) remained. Then as I gazed it began slowly to fade away, just like a dioramic dissolving view.*

Mr Walker received a telegram while having breakfast saying that Oastler had died in Harrogate at 6am that morning and he was required to help with the funeral. There are many newspaper articles of sightings at the Hall (16 November 1925, 12 May 1927, 15 July 1927) and there are many more recent encounters (summer 2002, October 2004 and December 2004). One of the local community police officers was being given a tour of the Hall, went into the red couch bedroom in the Georgian wing and ran out panicking. He was unable to explain what was the matter.

17

THE HAND OF GLORY, DANBY

The parish of Danby in Yorkshire possessed one of these hands. It was something that superstitious burglars considered an essential part of their kit until the end of the 18th century. The hand belonged to a gibbeted murderer. It was cut off and the blood squeezed out. The hand was then embalmed for up to eight weeks in a solution of saltpetre, salt and pepper, before being dried in the sun. A candle was made from a number of ingredients such as hanged man's fat, virgin wax and Lapland sesame. This candle was then thrust between the dead fingers and lit when a burglar broke into a house. This magical hand was supposed to open locks, render the thief invisible and send the household into a deep sleep. First of all the burglar had to recite the following words:

Let those who rest more deeply sleep, let those awake, their vigils keep, oh, hand of glory, shed thy light, direct us to our spoil tonight.

It was believed that the candle's spell could only be broken by putting out the flame with skimmed milk or blood, and then the household would wake. The most famous site where the hand of glory was used was at the Old Spital Inn on Bowes Moor, between Barnard Castle and Brough. Around

THE HAND OF GLORY

The parish of Danby, Yorkshire, possessed a Hand of Glory, a device which superstitious burglars considered an essential part of their kit until the early 19th century. The hand was that of a gibbeted criminal; after the blood was squeezed out, the hand was embalmed for two weeks in a solution of saltpetre, salt and pepper, before being dried in the sun. A candle was made from a number of curious ingredients such as hanged man's fat, wax, and a substance called Lapland sesame. The resulting confection was thrust between the dead fingers, and lit when the burglar broke into a house. The hand was supposed to open locks, render the thief invisible, and send the household into a drugged sleep, particularly when the burglar recited:

Let those who rest
more deeply sleep;
Let those awake
their vigils keep;
Oh, Hand of Glory,
shed thy light;
Direct us to our
spoil tonight.

It was believed that the candle's spell could be broken only by putting out its flames with blood or skimmed milk; then the household would awake.

HAND OF GLORY *This grisly relic is displayed in Whitby Museum, Yorkshire*

1800 a traveller dressed in women's clothes appeared at the Inn, and asked if she could sleep a while by the fire. A maid noticed men's trousers under the skirt, and realised something was afoot, so she pretended she was asleep. She watched the traveller produce the hand of glory and light the candle. He then opened the locked door for his accomplices. The maid jumped up and slammed the door shut, locking the thieves out. She rushed upstairs to wake the landlord and his family but could not wake them. By this time the thieves were breaking down the door. In desperation the maid threw a bowl of skimmed milk over the hand, and the family woke immediately. The thieves promised they would leave if they could reclaim their hand of glory. The inn keeper's reply was a shot from his musket, which sent them on their way.

18

THE BARGUEST OR
BLACK DOG

By tradition, almost every wilderness has its supernatural inhabitants, from the Devil, giants, ghosts and fairies to horrible animals such as Yorkshire's Barguest or black dog. These wild creatures roam not only the hills of Yorkshire, but also the snickleways of York, terrifying anyone who sets eyes on them, especially in the dark. They are normally larger than life, with red or yellow saucer-like eyes, shaggy coats, and often dragging chains.

Different communities had different black dogs. For example, in the district of Bent Ing outside Bradford in the 1890s, half-a-dozen girls sat in a row on the bridge, waiting for dark to fall so that they could terrify each other with stories about the Bloody Tongue. This was a great dog with staring red eyes, and a tail as big as the branch of a tree, and a lolling tongue that dripped blood. When he drank from the beck the water ran red right past the bridge. Nobody had ever seen him – apart from one girl, but she saw him in the shadows every night, so that didn't count. He lived only as a rumour or legend, but in the hands of a less sensitive writer, Bloody Tongue would have been recorded as just another instance of the black dog phenomenon.

This fearsome creature, this ghost dog, was once thought to haunt a nearby gorge called Trollers Gill, near

Appletreewick in Yorkshire. A local story recorded in 1881 tells how a foolhardy man went to the gorge at midnight. His body was found by shepherds the next day, and according to a contemporary ballad, 'Marks were impressed on the dead man's breast, but they seemed not by mortal hand.'

In their heyday, legends such as these helped to reinforce established values, or to sanction new ones. Early Christian

149

priests probably encouraged the legends about men being turned to stone on a Sunday, partly to keep their churches full, and partly to discourage people from visiting sites linked with older, pagan religion.

The legends also had a practical function. Families living in wild and remote parts of Yorkshire needed to discourage their children from wandering alone on to the moors. So they filled these lonely places with fearful creatures who roamed the hills, scratched children to death with their long claws, ate their flesh and drank their blood and, when the foul feast was over, hung their skins to dry in their caves.

Most of the pagan myths and legends, such as headless horsemen and phantom funerals, have long been laid to rest, but the black dog is still very much alive and he's reported to be seen by many people to this day. I know of a senior lecturer in Psychology at the Centre of Anomalous Psychological Process at University College, Northampton, who has a PhD in psychology and had an encounter as a child. To quote Simon Sherwood '…the year was about 1974. I had been in bed at couple of hours. I awoke to hear a patter of feet. I looked up thinking it was my dog, but to my terror I saw a massive black animal, probably with horns but perhaps ears, galloping along the landing towards my bedroom. I tried to scream but I found it impossible. The creature's eyes were bright yellow and as big as saucers. The animal got to my bedroom door and then vanished as quick as it had appeared.'

Another theory about these black dogs is that they are harbingers of death and anyone who has the misfortune to have one of these creatures cross their path will be dead in a few days. But I believe that Simon is still alive and well and still lecturing in Northampton.

19

TEMPLE NEWSAM, LEEDS

Like Bolling Hall, Temple Newsam also became a museum and art gallery and was bought by Leeds Corporation in 1922. This magnificent red-brick mansion has often been referred to as the Hampton Court of Yorkshire. In mediaeval times the property belonged to the Knights Templar. In 1908 the present building was the home of the famous writer of ghost stories, Lord Halifax. One night when he was fast asleep he was woken by the ghost of a blue lady who appeared at the foot of his bed. She was wearing a lace shawl and underneath it was a blue dres. For all we know this ghostly incident may have caused him to start writing his famous ghost stories. There are various ghosts in this building: the ghost of a Knight Templar has been seen in the south wing, terrible agonised screams are often heard, cleaners who work in the building will never work alone at night and they often talk of a lady wearing a long flowing dress who brushes past them while they work on the 13 steps. There is also poltergeist activity in the building and many people report the sound of heavy furniture being moved about in the bedrooms, but when they go to investigate nothing is ever out of place.

Probably the most famous inhabitant of Temple Newsam is Henry, Lord Darnley. He was the second husband of Mary Queen of Scots and he was also the father of King James I of

Great Britain. Darnley was a vain and stupid man and Mary and he fell out in a big way. One night he and some knights burst into Mary's rooms in Holyrood Palace and stabbed to death Mary's Italian secretary David Rizzio. Eight months later, in February 1567, Darnley caught smallpox, and because of the danger to their baby son he was persuaded by Mary to convalesce alone in an old house at Kirk O' Fields in Edinburgh. Mary visited him on the evening of 9 February, but returned to Holyrood the same night in order to attend a wedding. During that night the house was blown up and Darnley's body was found the next morning in the grounds. He had been strangled.

Perhaps the ghost of a small boy who often steps from a cupboard in the Darnley Room is the ghost of Mary's murdered husband – perhaps this is the place where he was happiest and that is why he still haunts the place to this day.

20

THE BLACK BULL AT HAWORTH

The name 'Brontë' conjures up a vision of three talented sisters who wrote books and lived in a bleak parsonage in the remote moorland village of Haworth in Yorkshire. These sisters were Charlotte, Emily and Anne. But there was another sibling, a gifted brother, who always lived in the shadow of his sisters. His name was Patrick Branwell Brontë. Branwell, as he was generally called, was born in the village of Thornton, three miles west of Bradford. The family moved to Haworth in April 1820, their father Patrick becoming the vicar of Haworth. Branwell was red headed, short-sighted, slightly built and gifted in many ways. He played the flute and the organ, could read and write both Latin and Greek, and was also ambidextrous. He sketched, painted in oils and wrote stories and poetry. He had a fine sense of humour and was an extrovert. He loved his drink and spent most of his time in the local pub, the Black Bull. He also had a love for the moors around his home and they were an escape from the everyday view of the grim graveyard at Haworth, which contained over 40,000 bodies. Branwell had a fascination for ghosts, and grew up with stories like the Horton Guytrash, which took the form of a great black dog with horrid eyes and chains around its neck. Horton was a village very close to Branwell's birthplace. In fact his uncle,

Hugh Brontë, is said to have gone forth to lay the spirits carrying a sword and Bible. Ghostly visitations also troubled one of the Reverend Brontë's curates, a Mr Hodgson. In 1835 Branwell, although sceptical, was asked to test the truth of the curate's ghost story by spending a night in the curate's house. Branwell accepted the challenge. One night's experience was quite enough and Branwell never went there again.

Little is known about the history of the Black Bull. As far as we know it has always been a pub and a hotel and it goes back at least 300 years. This was the place in which Branwell Brontë drank away his health, and the pub has been regarded by many as being largely responsible for his downfall. He also took drugs and bought his opium in the apothecary's shop across the cobbled street. While his sisters were writing their

novels in the parsonage behind, Branwell was spending his time drinking in the pub. Their father, the vicar, was most upset by the antics of his son 'the black sheep of the family'.

Mrs Chadwick, author of *In the footsteps of the Brontë's*, talked to many of the Haworth residents who knew the Brontës. When the landlord was taxed with having sent for Branwell, in order to entertain the guests, he replied, "I never sent for him at all, he came himself, hard enough". He admitted, however that sometimes the vicar or his daughter would call at the front door to inquire if Branwell was there, upon which occasions Branwell would jump through the kitchen window, or go through the back door, when the landlord would be able to give a satisfactory answer.

There are many eyewitness accounts of ghosts at the pub. A man dressed in a beige suit has been seen sitting at the bar, dark figures are often seen, usually out of the corner of the eye, glasses and ashtrays fly to the floor when there is no one around. There is a very interesting picture of the Brontë sisters with another figure that has been painted out. There is a bell by the fireplace in the corner of the room very near to this picture and the bell often rings of its own accord. Also, most mornings the light above the Brontë picture is turned round. Footsteps are often heard in the attic; a girl is heard crying outside in the car-park and room three is believed to be haunted by a maid. Most often seen is the figure of a man, always wearing a top hat, and often cigar-smoke is smelled at the same time. Who could this figure be? The landlord at the time of the Brontës was a little man called Jack Sugden, who always wore a top hat, but so did Branwell Brontë and he loved cigars.

I visited the pub and took part in a table tilting session in which I believe we got in contact with Branwell's father

Patrick, the vicar of Haworth, and we ascertained that Branwell Brontë still haunts the pub because his father will not forgive him for his sins and he believes that he will go to Hell. Hence the fact that he has chosen to stay around his favourite haunt, the Black Bull.

When I left the building at about five o'clock in the morning, I turned back and took some photographs of the churchyard, the parsonage and the Black Bull. Many weeks later when I looked at the pictures I noticed that the pub was completely surrounded by a snowstorm of orbs.

Branwell's ghost does not only haunt the Yorkshire moors. In 1978 the national newspapers printed a story from a restaurant in Haworth, where the owner said he had seen the ghost of Emily Brontë on 19 December, the day she died. He said he saw the ghost climb a staircase that had been

removed some time before. It was a small slim figure, who giggled and chuckled happily. The haunting had started some 12 years previously and he had been able to identify her from the portrait of the family. Possibly a more appropriate place for Emily's ghost to appear is on the moors that she loved so well, and indeed her ghost is supposed to haunt the path up to the waterfall, a sad figure who walks with bowed head. Just across the border the ruins of Wycoller Hall lie to the east of Burnley, amid the bleak moorland close to the Yorkshire boundary, and it is these moors that surround Haworth and make up Brontë country. Charlotte Brontë knew of one of the ghosts of Wycoller and described it in *Jane Eyre:* 'a lion-like creature with long hair, a huge head and with strange preter-canine eyes'. This of course is another local variety of the ghostly black dog called Guytrash Lightfoot, which at night roamed the lonely lanes and field paths that surround the remote ruins of the hall. Disaster or death for yourself or a loved one was sure to come to anyone unlucky enough to meet this terrifying creature. In *Jane Eyre* Mr Rochester had a painful fall from his horse after meeting such a figure.

FURTHER
RESEARCH

If you have been caught by the ghost-hunting bug after reading about our adventures in York-shire, the following publications and DVDs may be of interest to you.

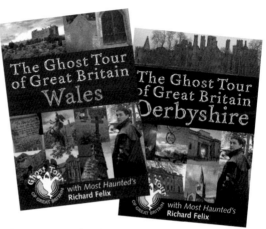

Books:

The Ghost Tour of Great Britain: Derbyshire with Richard Felix, Breedon Books, 2005.

The Ghost Tour of Great Britain: Wales with Richard Felix, Breedon Books, 2005.

Both of the above books are available from all good bookshops and may also be purchased direct from the publishers, Breedon Books, 3 The Parker Centre, Mansfield Road, Derby, DE21 4SZ, tel 01332 384 325, fax 01332 292 755, email sales@breedonpublishing.co.uk.

DVDs

This DVDs, as well as many others from the Ghost Tour of Great Britain, are available from shops in Derby and direct from the producers, Film Studios Ltd, 35 Eaton Bank, Duffield, Derby, DE56 4BJ, tel 01332 840 292. Order online at:
www.stephenlilley.co.uk

INDEX